FOLK-LORE AND CUSTOMS OF THE LAP-CHAS OF SIKHIM

FOLK-LORE AND CUSTOMS
OF THE
LAP-CHAS OF SIKHIM

C. DE BEAUVOIR STOCKS

GYAN

Published by

GYAN

Gyan Publishing House
5, Ansari Road
Daryaganj, New Delhi-110002
Phone: 011-47034999, 9811692060
E-mail: books@gyanbooks.com

Distribution Network
gyanbooks.com
India, USA, Canada, UK, Australia, France

ISBN : 978-81-212-3387-3 (PB)
First Published, Calcutta, 1925

2nd Impression 2020

Printed at: Gyan Press, Delhi.

Folk-Lore and Customs of the Lap-Chas of Sikhim
Author: C. De Beauvoir Stocks

ARTICLE No 23.

Folk-lore and Customs of the Lap-chas of Sikhim.

By C. DE BEAUVOIR STOCKS.

TABLE OF CONTENTS.

PREFACE.

Very little authentic information can be gathered from the literature that is extant on Sikhim and its original inhabitants, especially with regard to the folk-lore, religion, customs, or indeed regarding any other race in the Himalayas. The present work is the result of research on these particular lines of Lap-cha life. It was undertaken with the intention of getting more exact information, and the materials which are here published were collected in Sikhim itself during the greater part of 1925. Although it would be impossible to expect an exhaustive study of these subjects, even after long years of residence in the country, it may be safely said that the present paper presents a correct idea of Lap-cha characteristics, while it is hoped it also gives an accurate account of their folk-lore.

Many obstacles stand in the way of an anthropologist, who undertakes the study of a small and scattered tribe like that of the Lap-chas. They possess no indigenous literature, and but few educated men. The greatest difficulty is the language, which would require several years of preparatory study to acquire sufficient fluency in the Lap-cha idiom required, in order, not only to follow the conversation, but also to be able to write down the tales when they were dictated by these people, the *Rong*-folk. Therefore, if no specialization on this particular race be undertaken, the student must rely on the services of an interpreter.

These are not easily procurable, especially among the Lap-cha, and although on the whole an accurate translation is given by them which is quite sufficient for the purpose of anthropological research work, it would be beyond their ability to transmit "rhythm" correctly, to give the stylistical peculiarities of the original diction or to use antiquated expressions, etc.

This leads to another difficult question on which the student has to make a decision. The English which is spoken all over India, and which interpreters use, harmonizes little with the primeval matters discussed in these tales, or with their primitive psychology. It seems however, that it would be wrong to attempt to introduce quite arbitrarily some antiquated expressions. There are a great number of examples showing how unsuccessful this can be, unless it is in the hands of a really talented writer or poet. And in order to avoid this evident note of artificiality, the present tales have been left as far as possible in the form they were heard from the interpreters, except for the necessary correction in diction.

A comparative study of Lap-cha folk-lore with a definition of its real position in regard to its chief cause of influence, etc., is still not possible. The folk-lore of almost all the neighbours, even including the Tibetans, the most important among them, is completely unknown. This circumstance is of still greater importance when we consider that the Lap-cha is living much intermixed with the people of Nepal, Northern Bengal, Bhutan, etc., and is naturally much exposed to their influence, which is considerable when it is remembered that these people belong to a state of much higher culture than the Rong-folk.

The books to which references have been given are chiefly those dealing with information in all its branches, and are therefore, of an encyclopædical nature. These will give guidance to a student in bibliographical matters. They are Hastings' "*Encyclopædia of Religion*," J. Frazer's "*Folk-lore in the Old Testament*," and a few others, such as Gubernatis's "*Zoological Mythology*," etc.

I shall feel very glad if this small contribution will be of any use to those interested in anthropological research work, and especially should some student think it worth while continuing a study of the Lap-cha and other Himalayan peoples.

In conclusion, I have to express my thanks to Major F. M. Bailey, the Political Officer in Gangtok, for his great help and kindness, and to Mr. W. Ivanow for his valuable suggestions concerning the technique of this paper. Also to Paul Babu who organized my first tour, and to Dora Guest, the wife of the *lama* Ate in Tumun, who was with me for seven months, and to all the numerous Lap-cha *kazis*, *mandals*, *lamas*, compounders and peasants who assisted me in my work, and who made my visits to Sikhim so enjoyable.

DARJEELING, BENGAL: C. DE B. S.
March, 1926.

INTRODUCTION.

1. A brief note on the Geography and History of Sikhim.

Just a concise account will be given first of all denoting the general position with the natural boundaries of Sikhim. This small State is under British protection, and lies on the North of Bengal in the East Himalayas. It is bounded on the West by Nepal, on the North and East by Tibet, with a small part of the South-East end touching Bhutan. A clear explanation of both the physical features and of the events of the country are given in the *Imperial Gazetteer of India*, Vol. XXII, New Edition (Oxford, 1908) from which work the following quotation was obtained (p. 365) :—

"The main axis of the Himalayas, which runs east and west, forms the boundary between Sikhim and Tibet. The Singalila and Chola ranges, which run southwards from the main chain, separate Sikhim from Nepal on the west, and from Tibet and Bhutan on the east. From the eastern flank of the Singalila range rise the great snow peaks of Kinchin-junga (28,146 feet). It throws out a second spur terminating at Tendong. The Chola range which is much loftier than that of Singalila, leaves the main chain at the Dongkya mountain; it is pierced by several passes, the most frequented of which are the Tangkar La (16,000 feet), Natu La (14,200 feet), and Jelep La (14,390). Over the last named comes practically the whole trade between Bengal and Tibet. From the north-west face of the Dongkya mountain an immense spur takes off, and runs first west and then south-west to Kinchinjunga, forming the watershed of all the remote sources of the Tista river. These basins have a southward slope, being broad at the top where they leave the watershed, and gradually contracting like a fan from its rim to its handle, in the Tista valley near Pashok. The rivers are very rapid, and generally run in deep ravines, the ascent from the bank for the first few hundred feet being almost precipitous."

It will be noticed that a great many of these mountains and rivers are mentioned in the Lap-cha mythology, and appear in the Creation myths, whilst they are also spoken of in numerous folk tales (see tales, Nos. I, II, III, V, VI, VII, XXXI, etc.).

The Lap-cha or Rong-folk, being but a small tribe, and having only a very primitive state of civilization, do not possess written records. Allusion some day may possibly be found in connection with them in Chinese annals or in some

Tibetan legends, but so far, they remain unstudied. References regarding Sikhim do not appear earlier than roughly—150 years ago. The following is another quotation from the *Imperial Gazetteer of India* (p. 367) giving some of the historical events:—

"Sikhim was known to early European travellers, such as Horace della Penna, and Samuel van de Putte, under the name Bramashon, while Bogle called it Demojong. Local tradition asserts that the ancestors of the Rajas of Sikhim originally came from the neighbourhood of Lhasa in Tibet. About the middle of the seventeenth century, the head of the family was named Puntso Namgyal; and to him repaired three Tibetan monks, professors of the Nyingmapa (or 'red cap' sect of Buddhism), who were disgusted at the predominance of the Gelukpa sect in Tibet. These lamas, according to Mr. Edgar's Report, succeeded in converting the Lepchas of Sikhim to their own faith, and in making Puntso Namgyal Raja of the country. The avatars of two of these lamas are now the heads, respectively, of the two great monasteries of Pemiongchi and Tassiding (p. 368). In 1788 the Gurkhas invaded Sikhim in the governorship of the Morang, and only retired in 1789, on the Tibetan government ceding to them a piece of territory at the head of the Koti pass. But in 1792, on a second invasion of Tibetan territory by the Gurkhas, an immense Chinese army advanced to the support of the Tibetans, defeated the Gurkhas, and dictated terms to them almost at the gates of Katmandu.

On the breaking out of the Nepal war in 1814, Major Latter at the head of a British force occupied the Morang, and formed an alliance with the Raja of Sikhim who gladly seized the opportunity of revenging himself on the Gurkhas. At the close of the war in 1816, the Raja was rewarded by a considerable accession of territory which had been ceded to the British by Nepal. In February 1835, the Raja granted the site of Darjeeling to the British, and received a pension of Rs. 3,000 per annum in lieu of it."

To this may be added that according to Lap-cha tradition the following kings reigned apparently at the same time in different parts of the country, Tur-ve, Tur-ayek, Tur-sang-pono, and Tur-sung. The Rong-folk history is very obscure, and it was only when these four had died, their places were taken by treasurers, secretaries, and headmen. At the present day, all villages are governed by a '*kazi*.'[1] He is the man who ranks next to the Maharaja, and is a land-owner, then next to him comes the '*mandal*,' the village headman.[2]

According to another legend which I heard at Kabi, a

---

[1] From 'qādī,' an Arabic term.

[2] A Khasura term (see *Imperial Gazetteer*, p. 372).

village in the Lap-cha reserve, the first Lap-cha chief was of divine origin; and Tikung-tek was the sixth in direct descent. He performed the duties of a *Bong-thing*, his wife Nikong-gnal being a Mun.[1] During the life-time of Je-khyé-bumen or Ket-boomse, who was an influential Tibetan, he lived at Namphyn, daily working at Ringchum. One day, Je-khyé-bumen passing through Sikhim on his way south, sought Tikung-tek, and praying to him, asked for the gift of children. Swearing eternal amity, Tikung-tek promised him three. After they were born, Je-khyé-bumen returned to give thanks to Tikungtek. At Karbi, near Gangtok, nine stones were erected to mark the place where they held their covenant.[2] A Chinaman was decapitated, and an oath was sworn over his blood, that the Tibetans and the Lap-cha should never fight, and that Je-khyé-bumen's second son, Mi-tpon-rab, the 'leader of men' would be the head of the family of the future Sikhim rulers. The alliance is said to have been formed chiefly because Jekhyé-bumen had the conversion of the Rong-folk to Buddhism in prospect.

On the fifteenth day of the ninth month (by the Tibetan calendar) the Lap-cha worship at Karbi, offering *chi*, the national drink, rice (*zo*), Indian corn (*ta-fa*), fish (*gnu*), birds (*fo*), sugarcane (*mut pa-am*), and flowers (*rip*). These offerings are placed on plantain leaves (*kur-dong nyom*) resting on a bamboo carpet in front of the altar to the north of the nine stones facing the Himalaya Mountains. They are the representation of the Lapcha crops, and it is believed this ceremony will entail good harvests, and bring plentiful hunting and fishing. This service is held by all the Rong-folk, whether they go to Karbi or not. Even the present Maharaja, H.H. Sir Tashi Namgyal, holds the service outside his palace at Gangtok, he being a descendant of De-jong.Gyalpe or Chogel-Penche-Namgyal.[3]

The Sikhim Maharajas are therefore Tibetan, and though the early kings in that country are said to have come of an Indian origin, no real history of Tibet was written previous to the seventh century. The first Sikhim Raja, Puntso Namgyal is descended from Zhal-nga-guru-Tasche, whose son Jekhyébumen was the man who consulted Grandfather Tikungtek and who, with his wife Nikong-gnal, are the first two ancestors the Lap-cha claim as their forefathers.[4]

Some of the Maharajas' wives, Maharanis, as they are termed, have been Lap-cha. Deba-sam-serpa, a Lap-cha, from Tinki-jong in the N.W. was the second wife of Tensung Namgyal, whilst the young nun whom Gyurme Namgyal, the

---

[1] See note 7 to *Folk-lore*, I.

[2] Called Long-chok, i.e. the Standing Stones.

[3] See note 4 to *Creation Myths*, IV.

[4] Genealogical Tree showing descent of the Sikhim Maharajas :—

fourth Sikhim Raja, married, belonged to the Tak-chungtar family at Sing-Jyang near Dubde.

Tikung-tek and Nikung-gnal are said to be still living in the Yahaun valley which lies under the slopes of the Kong-chin-chu. The Lap-cha believes that were everything destroyed by another flood, these two would only have to be visited in order to create all in the world again.

Though the Lap-cha is very loyal, I have heard him say, " we Rong-folk have no ruler as the Maharaja in Gangtok is in reality a Tibetan."

2. The Lap-cha or Rong-folk, their ethnical type and language.

An anthropological study of the Lap-cha[1] tribe has never been undertaken. In this respect few of the Himalayan tribes are known, and it is impossible to define the Lap-cha's original home, or to give his relation with his neighbours. The *Imperial Gazetteer* contains more complete information on this subject than any other work, and this is contained in the following few lines: "The Lepchas claim to be the autochthones of Sikhim proper. Their physical

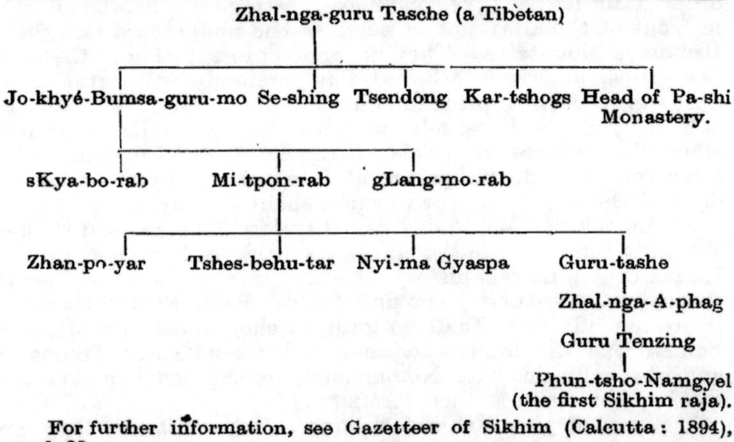

For further information, see Gazetteer of Sikhim (Calcutta: 1894), pp. 1–38.

[1] The local pronunciation is Lap-cha or Lap-che (never Lepcha, which one hears so often pronounced), and is of a Nepalese derivation. Lap-cha is derived from a word in the Parbatiya dialect of Nepal, meaning 'lap'—*speech*, and 'cha'—*unintelligible*, i.e. the *unintelligible speakers*, a contemptuous term referring to the tribe not adopting the Parbatiya language.

The term '*Rong-pa*' is often used meaning the *dwellers in the steep country*, whilst they also use the term '*Mong-pa*' which means the *dwellers in the lower country*. See *Gazetteer of Sikhim*, op. cit., p. 39.

Pa-lit—a Lap-cha. Kasseon (N. Bengal).

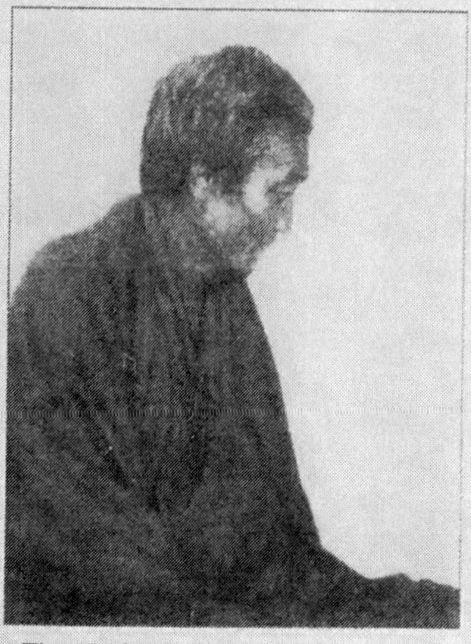

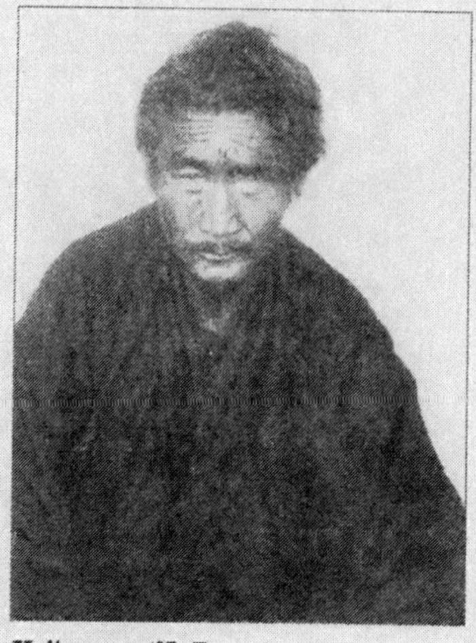

The *Na-ju-mo's* husband—a Lap-cha. Kalimpong (N. Bengal).

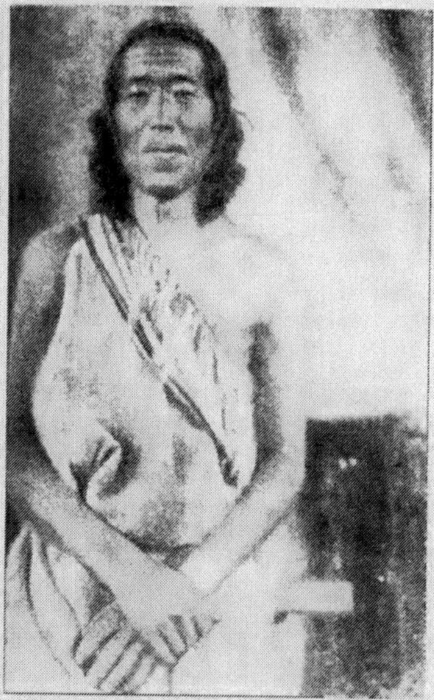

Chyungay—a 'Sharabu'—(hunter).

Lang-dang (Sikkim).

Gynda—a Lap-cha forest officer.

Lang-dang (Sikkim).

Full Lap-cha dress. Gangtok (Sikkim).

The *Kazi* of Mangen's Wife and Sister in Tibetan dress (note doll).

De-lau. Rinchenpong (Sikkim).

A "*na-ju-mo*" is the Lap-cha female exorciser who inspired by dancing predicts. Kalimpong, Bengal.

A young Lap-cha girl.

Mangen (Sikkim).

A Lap-cha woman.

Tumun (Sikkim).

Pa-sen (*De-bies* wife).

Rinchenpong (Sikkim).

characteristics stamp them as being members of the Mongolian race, while certain peculiarities of language and religion render it probable that the tribe is a very ancient colony from southern Tibet. (The language they speak belongs to the Tibeto-Burman family. To this also belong the languages of Bhotia, Limbu, Murmi, Mangar, Khambu and Newar.)"

The Lap-cha has but a very limited literature, consisting almost entirely of translations from Tibetan religious books. The alphabet was invented in the seventeenth century, few people knowing it at the present time, the language not being taught in all the local schools. A grammar was written by General Mainwaring,[1] but a proper definition of its affinity to other branches of the same order cannot be clearly established till the local dialects have been investigated, and more is known about Himalayan philology, which is still at present, a matter of the future.

Later, I hope to publish a paper giving an analysis of the head and height measurements of the various people whom I found in different parts of Sikhim, comparing the Lap-cha race with others.

3. A Summary of both tours in Sikhim.

April 15th–June 3rd, 1925. First Tour.

From Kalimpong.

April 15th	Rissisoum.
April 16th–18th	Kasseon.
April 19th-20th	Rhenock.
April 21st	Pakyong.
April 22nd–24th	Gangtok.
April 25th-26th	Dickhu.
April 27th-May 3rd	Mangen.
May 4th–6th	Lang-dang.
May 7th–9th	Ling-them.
May 10th–17th	Sindhik.
May 18th-19th	Toon.
May 20th	Sindhik.
May 21st-22nd	Dickhu.
May 23rd	Phodang.
May 24th-25th	Phensang.
May 26th	Kabi.
May 27th–30th	Gangtok.
June 1st	Pakyong.
June 2nd	Rhenock.
June 3rd	Kalimpong.

1 Mainwaring, A Grammar of the Rong (Lep-cha) language, Calcutta, 1876.

November 9th–December 16th. Second Tour.

From Kalimpong.

Nov. 9th	Lopchu.
Nov. 10th–12th	Darjeeling.
Nov. 13th	Badamtan.
Nov. 14th–15th	Namchi.
Nov. 16th	Chakung.
Nov. 17th-18th	Rinchenpong.
Nov. 19th-20th	Pemiongchi.
Nov. 21st–23rd	Kewsing.
Nov. 24th	Temi.
Nov. 25th-26th	Song.
Nov. 27th–Dec. 4th	Tumun.
Dec. 5th–9th	Dickhu.
Dec. 10th–13th	Gangtok.
Dec. 14th	Shemdong.
Dec. 15th	Rungpo.
Dec. 16th	Kalimpong.

I. FOLK-LORE OF THE RONG-FOLK.

1. The Mythology and Religion of the Rong-folk as reflected in their tales.

Tibetan lamaism was introduced into Sikhim three centuries ago and is now regarded as the official religion. There have been many attempts to study this and to give a brief summary of its doctrine; the reader may be referred to the literature given below for information.[1] It is difficult to determine the extent Buddhist influence has had on Lap-cha psychology, but it is clear that the pre-Buddhist religion is not entirely dead: a collection of tales, like those at hand, give sufficient evidence to this effect.

The most difficult task is to separate the pure Lap-cha beliefs from the "loan-myths." In this country, not only Tibetan Buddhist ideas are disseminated, but with them probably the motives of Tibetan folk-lore have also spread. To these must be added the natural borrowings of tales from the peoples of Bhutan and Nepal, with whom the Lap-chas have now much mixed. Perhaps some of the ideas were imported from India, directly or indirectly, and of late, Christian missionaries even can be ranked among the contributors. A clear idea of what can be called the original Lap-cha religion will probably be only possible when an exhaustive study of all the tales and customs of the different races inhabiting this corner of the Himalayas is taken, including the Rong-folks, immediate neighbours. Till this is done, the only possible way to deal with the Lap-cha tales is to treat them as being entirely original—with the exception of those that bear obvious traces of Buddhist or foreign influence.

In these stories, one can trace two distinct phases of Lap-cha mentality. What probably belongs to an earlier period, or to some species of more primitive culture absorbed by the Lap-cha, is the atmosphere of animistic beliefs. Humans occupy here only a secondary position, and the animals, insects, and

---

[1] See L. A. Waddell, *The Buddhism of Tibet* (London, 1895): also his articles in the *Gazetteer of Sikhim* (Calcutta, 1894), *Lamaism in Sikhim*, pp. 241–392, also Hastings', *Encyclopædia of Religion*, vol. VII, pp. 784–789 and Ronaldshay, *The Land of the Thunderbolt* (London, 1924).

Though these works by no means exhaust the subject, they give sufficient information for the elementary idea of research work among the Lap-cha. In my collection there are several stories that were obviously inspired by the pupil of some missionary; one of them (heard at Mangen) gives the Genesis version of the story of Adam and Eve. The other, told by Dorjejimbo lama at Kewsing repeats the same but with still more detail.

plants receive the whole attention of the narrator. The second phase belongs to a culture of a much more advanced group, and deals chiefly with heroes and demons. Both elements are prominent, and it would be unfair to treat the more primitive ideas as being merely the incidental survivals of an earlier state of Lap-cha mentality.

1. *The cosmogony*, as gathered from the creation myths and heroic tales, appears to be simple. The earth, like an earthen pot, floats on a space of infinite water (VI), or is supported by a tortoise (IV). Beneath the water there is a region of fire, and under that there is a world of wind, in which the spirit of the earthquake lives (I, i). The process of creation is not detailed, and apparently Lap-cha psychology takes more interest in the creation of plants, animals, and spirits than in the origin of the universe.

There is no explicit mention of the world under the earth being associated with the Hell of Christianity; this latter idea seems to be absent, and demons settle on the earth. *A-nok* (XXIV, 12) is mentioned but its meaning is not clear.

The sky receives much more attention. We have the story of its gradual adornment by clouds (I, 10). Originally there were two suns (IX, i; XXVI, 4), but one of them was killed by a toad (IX, 3).[1]

Above the sky there is the *Rum-lyang*, the country of the Gods, the ancestral spirits, etc., who are known as the *Rum* (*lyang* means country). In this Olympus or Walhalla (not a Paradise in the Christian sense), life is experienced in the usual way: there are families of kings amongst others, many animals, and there is plenty of rivalry, envy and treachery (cf. the story of *Ati-azyak*, XXVI). The *Rum* do not seem to be fond of staying there eternally, the chance of being re-incarnated on the earth stirs up quite a lively competition among the brothers of *Ati-azyak*. The *Rum* often look down to the earth (V; XXVI, 2; XXVIII, 2), etc. In order to be re-born on the earth one must die leaving the *Rum* country, (XXVI; XXVIII). The

---

[1] This motive is also found in the stories of other races, e.g. the Meiteis who tell of a slave, becoming exhausted through continual day and night work, and having no rest, kills one of the suns (Hastings' *Encyclopædia*, vol. VIII, p. 78). The Malays also believe there were three original suns—a husband with a wife and child (ibid.), one of which devours the other two. At Pemionchi, Gensay Potet explained that the sun and moon were regarded as a brother and sister (they are usually identified with the deities Takbo-thing and Nazong-gnyu), but there is some difference of opinion as to which is the male or female; it appears however that it is to the sun that the feminine sex is usually attributed. According to some tales heard at Darjeeling and at Pemionchi there were originally seven, or even eight suns and eight moons, and the water-frog (instead of the toad) shot all of them except one. At Namchi it was mentioned that the figure which is seen in the moon is a red-cherry tree, under which two orphan children are living, a boy and a girl.

hero descends either in the form of a hail-stone (V; XXVI), which is swallowed by a woman and impregnates her, or some animal, in which case it is swallowed as a hail-stone by a female creature of the same species (XXVI, 2; XXVIII, 2).

Strange is the belief that men and animals can fly up to the *Rum* country from the earth without dying (see: *Ati-azyak* with his wives, XXVI, 13; his horse, XXVI, 13; and the squirrel, XX, 6).

It is also interesting to note that there is the additional idea of an intermediate country that lies between the earth and the *Rum-lyang* (I, 12; XXVI, 2; XXVIII, 1). It is sometimes called *Tiamtan*, *Sari-rung-dong-chen* or *Siri-nong-dong-chen*. Most probably this simply refers to the idea of the outside world—beyond the insignificant limits of the Lap-cha geography

2. The conception of *gods* is vague, and apparently it had not attained maturity when it was superseded by Buddhism. As the cosmological myths are almost silent on this point, it is difficult to form any clear idea. Added to this, the original names have probably been forgotten; some of these are purely descriptive, like '*It-mo*,' "the ancient mother," others are of a Tibetan origin, the name *Tashey-takbo-thing* being the name which is applied to Padmasambhava, the apostle of Buddhism, and which in more modern circumstances is also applied to the Christian God-Creator.

It appears that there were five original deities: *It-mo* and her husband *Pa sandi*[1]; their children *Nazong-ngyu* and *Takbo-thing*,[2] and *Tashey-thing* the son of the former (VII, 1). In these creative power is attributed to the female deities, *It-mo* and *Nazong-ngyu*. Most probably these family relationships are simply the primitive expression of the conception of the deities' 'attributes' or 'aspects.' The mother *It-mo* in her chthonic state is probably the same as *Nazong-ngyu* or *Nikung-gnal* in their aspect of the living force of vegetable or animal nature, or as a solar deity.

The idea of the primeval 'father' is not clearly expressed. Here we probably have to deal with the idea of the 'ruler' of the world, whose duty it is to maintain the order of things after their creation. Nothing can be said about the nature of the Creator-father *Pa-sandi*; in one of his aspects, he is known under many different names; he may have been known as a

[1] The latter is only mentioned once (II, 1), and as apparently there is much confusion between the functions of him and his son, Takbo-thing, it would be difficult to establish his real nature.

[2] In his different aspects, or perhaps re-incarnations, he is also known as Tikung-tek, Foog-rong (VII, 1), Pudung-thing (VI) Sometimes he is regarded as the first man, or at least as the progenitor of the Lap-cha (VI). Most probably it is he and his wife Nikong-gnal who appear as the 'Grandfather' and the 'Grandmother' in the heroic tales (XXIV).

lunar deity.[1] But the most popular form of the same male principle is *Tashey-thing*.

This latter is often therianthropic, he appears as a fox (XXVII), or as the husband of a she-boar (VIII), when he is probably represented in the same form: he is also represented as the husband of a partridge or a quail (VII). These particular animals are used in the folk-lore of many nations as the impersonation of the corn-spirit.[2] But *Tashey-thing* is connected more with animals than plants, probably on the account that hunting formerly was the chief source of subsistence among the Rong-folk. It is he who establishes fish sacrifices (IV, 2; VIII, 4), those of a pig (VIII, 3), and those of fish and fruit during the sowing and harvest times (IV, 3), etc., which obviously have nothing to do with Buddhism as this latter has no blood-sacrifice. According to more modern beliefs, probably under Buddhist influence, *Tashey-thing* has no father or mother and rises, like all Hindu gods from a flower. His idols are made of brass or copper, in the form of a man having a big body, and holding a stick in his left hand, his right hand being uplifted. He has a moustache and wears a pointed cap. The Lap-cha believes he is now flying over the snow mountains.

One of the most noticeable points in this primitive religion is the conception of the *Bong-thing*, who might be called a shaman, a medicine man or an exorciser. He was, in the first place, believed to be the son of a goddess who was sent to relieve the humans from the tortures of the demons, and to be an intermediary between the *Rum* and the humans (I, 11). Quite in agreement with animistic ideas, the Lap-chas make the Creator send a variety of plants and insects for this purpose. These are not satisfactory, and eventually the real *Bong-thing* descends from above, though it is not clear if he is in human form or not. The adventures of this Saviour are not a success also; he finds the *Mung* or evil spirits so numerous that they occupy most of the trees and mountains and rocks, etc. (I, II). And far from overpowering them, this representative of the deity has to beat a hasty retreat, and being caught by the demons has to agree to rather humiliating terms: he makes a covenant with these evil beings that they will leave the humans in peace as long as they are propitiated by blood-sacrifices (I, 12).[3]

---

[1] See above, note 1.

[2] Cf. *Golden Bough*, vol. vii, pp. 295–303.

[3] When a man is ill, a *Bon-thing* is called who at once burns incense to know whether it is the *Rum* or the *Mung* who are troubling the sick person. Then by counting his rosary and throwing dice, he discovers what is troubling the patient, and sacrifices. In the case of a woman being ill, a *Mun* is called, a woman who sings and who calls up the *Rum*. The severity of the illness indicates the form of sacrifice, sometimes it seems only necessary to propitiate the evil demon with a basket filled with

A Lap-cha *basti* in the Rung-nyo (Tista) Valley.

A Lap-cha *basti* at Bom (N. Bengal).

3. *Demons.*—This is all that need be said about the gods, but much more must be mentioned in connection with evil spirits. From their fantasy and psychology every race creates its supernatural beings, and it is remarkable to notice that the Indians and Tibetans between whom the Lap-cha lives, possess such an unrivalled and inexhaustible stock of demons, monsters, evil and vile spirits, witches, devils, etc., compared with whom the deities pale into insignificance.

The same 'mother' or 'mothers' of the universe appear to be indefatigable in giving birth to spirits of illness, and misfortune, demons, etc. The heroic tales are filled with demoniacal beings, ogres, etc. The unhealthy jungles with dangerous animals, the frightening natural phenomena, etc., receive the attentions of a particular demon in every locality, each of whom it would be impossible to mention individually.[1] Demons abound everywhere, the world in its original state seems to be full of evil. There seems also to be no trace of the idea of the supremacy of the good, the forces of evil are kept in subordina-

---

small bamboo stems containing rice, millet seeds, and grain. I found one like this in the jungle near Tumun, and also heard a girl say, who was describing her illness to a friend: "Yes, I was very bad, it cost us two bullocks..." The exorcisers who dance as well as falling into a trance, and praying are (1) a man who is termed a *Pau,* and (2) a woman who is called a *Na-ju-mo.* They both find out which demon it is who is troubling the invalid by throwing four or eight eggs on the ground, pronouncing the name of a demon while they throw rice on the broken eggs. Should the rice be covered, it is the demon's name they have just then been pronouncing, and they know it is he who has to be propitiated. I have not been able to find out if her name *Na-ju-mo,* is the same as the word used for the Lap-cha goddess of Pre-creation, *Na-zong-nyo* (who is evidently the same as the goddess called Nazong-ngyu in the Creation myths); *Nun-zong-nyo* or *Na-grong-nyo.* I saw this ceremony at Kalimpong last September. The *Na-ju-mo* erected an altar, on which she placed bowls of food for the various gods. It was also decorated with many rice 'mandala cones' as they are termed in the *Gazetteer of Sikhim* (see pp. 274–320), but which the Lap-chas exhibit as a phallic offering. The *Na-ju-mo* started singing in Tibetan after she had whirled round, and then repeated while in a trance what the spirits had said to her. She only gave an hour's demonstration, and then stopped as she said that *Mut-li* (the god of fortune) was cursing her.

[1] The *Rot-mung* was said to haunt Mt. Tendong, and to take a toll of two lives every year. The demon is represented as having a hooked beak. I also passed a cascade falling over a rock from Tumun to Dickhu, and was told it was where the *Rung-nyo-ung-dut* lives. He is known to have caught people with an invisible chain and they die soon after. Where the Rung-nyo river meets the Dickhu river, on a rock, I once saw an offering to the *Rung-si-mung,* a demon who worries children and makes them cry out at night. Her form was made of mud, sitting amongst the gifts of eggs, rice, grain, etc., in a basket made of plaited bamboo. She is a demon who is always represented with an umbrella, which is depicted by small bamboo stems that are joined together with pieces of coloured threads. There is a great variety of different species of malignant beings; the generic name seems to be '*mung,*' but there are also the '*dut*' demons, while the female demons are '*sa-mu.*'

tion rather by magic than by the 'sacredness' of any religious act.

4. *Man.*—The creation of man, his position in the universe, and his relation to the gods and the demons, all remain without definite description. There are several accounts in which the first man appears either as the offspring of a supernatural mother (a fairy, cf. V), and a deity in animal form, or the first husband traps his wife like a bird (I, 13; IV, 1). This animal ancestry may be a survival of ancient totemistic ideas, just like the astonishing number of sacred insects and plants (especially different bamboo species, which are all prominent in the magical rites of resuscitation and rebirth, XXIV, 23; XXVI, 12).

Soon after his appearance, mankind multiplied to such an extent that he overcrowded the earth, and their number was reduced by the great flood (VI; VII). The Lap-chá has also a parallel of the story of the Tower of Babel (VII, 2). Both these myths appear however without any ethical comment Ethical matters, in fact, are not a strong point of the Lap-cha, and it is difficult to get even the principal features of their moral code.

The religious duties appear only in the form of sacrifices. No mention of temples or other places of worship is made, or of idols, etc. In these tales many references to religious details appear to be taken from Buddhism, and are given possibly as substitutes for earlier terms.

5. *Natural Myths.*—The Lap-cha universe is remarkably small, and their geography is limited. It seems as if they never dared leave their narrow valleys to view the outside world. The myths which are the most prominent seem to be connected with the solar or lunar theories. Numerous too, are the heroic legends.

Undoubtedly solar origin may be given to the myth of Nazong-ngyu and her brother-husband Takbo-thing (I, 3–7, 9; II). Parallels of this tale may be found in the different stories of many primitive nations. Its natural sequence is the story of the Cloud demon who is the son of *Nazong-ngyu* (II), who sits on the *sa-nyol*-tree growing out of *Nazong-ngyu*'s bracelet which she takes off at night (probably symbolising the disc of the sun).[1] This demon is shot by arrows (lightning), is dismembered and scattered.

In heroic tales (like that of the divine twins, XXIV), although the original myth became obscured or forgotten in them, natural symbolism has clear traces. The same may be said about the story of the hero who travels far to fetch the luminous flowers (XXVII), or the tale of Ga-bu's horse (XXV).

---

[1] Cf. Hastings' *Encyclopædia*, vol. 12, p. 68, where similar myths occur. The Eskimos, Cherokees, etc., are referred to. Many who were questioned in different parts of Sikhim said that Nazong-gnyu and Takbo-thing were the sun and moon.

The same solar myth appears also in the animal stories (IX). The lunar myth, separately from the solar, appears in the stories of killing the tiger who is celestial[1] (X). His skin is stretched from sunrise to sunset, and his flesh is scattered. Another story tells us how the celestial tiger is frightened by a toad, who is looked upon possibly as the animal who causes eclipses (XI).[2] The same celestial tiger is also frightened by an ass, probably another solar symbol, etc.[3]

In the heroic tales, Ati-azyak seems to be the most complete impersonation of a lunar deity. He fights the demons of darkness, until the fiery peacock of the day begins its dance and burns them. He is connected with two nymphs, Zer-yong and Konyong, the palace of the former is on the side of the sunrise, while the second one has it on the side of the sunset. The small detail is remarkable showing the double nature of these two nymphs: they are shown as both being benignant and demoniacal. Zer-yong appears not only as a beautiful maiden, but also as a monster having long tusks, one outstretched to the sky, and the other touching the earth, and long breasts, one hanging down, while the other is thrown over her shoulder (XXVI, 11). With these two, Ati-azyak disappears as soon as the demons of darkness are subdued, and his successor, miraculously born from a bamboo stem, takes charge of the world.

As releasing and stopping waters, killing the Serpent-King, *Paril-bu*, etc., are parts of this story, this tale may have been connected with the flood-legend (VI), where these acts are performed by the King Yong-li. Mythology may have given some remote reflection to the female '*dramatis personae*' of these heroic tales, especially in regard to the tale of the twins. But having only the materials of the present collection, it would be impossible and risky to enter the boundless fields of hypothesis.

2. An Analysis of the Lap-cha Folk-tales.

If taken as a specimen of folk-lore in general, these Lap-cha tales are remarkable in one sense—they are almost devoid of anything original. This is surprising when we consider the secluded life these people lead, who, up to a few decades ago, lived entirely isolated from the rest of the world. In these

---

1 The waning of the moon (as I heard at Pemionchi) is explained by this satellite being eaten by a tiger who eventually swallows it. But *Takbo-thing*, the lunar deity, cut him in two, so that the moon emerges after having been swallowed through the gap half-way through the tiger's body. In a tale I heard at Namchi it was told that the sun had borrowed money from the tiger, which he could not repay, and that in anger, the tiger swallows him.

2 The Karens of Burma believe eclipses are caused by frogs clipping the moon. Hastings' *Encyclopædia*, vol. i, p. 492.

3 Cf. ass in the tiger's skin. Gubernatis, op. cit., vol. i, p. 378.

tales not only ideas, but separate motives may be traced elsewhere.

This phenomenon however, can hardly be explained as occurring without foreign influence. The want of originality may be due to the result of Indian and Tibetan influence for many centuries. And India, although creating very few fresh ideas, has always had a supply of folk-lore, full of new patterns from the more western countries, from the Persian conquerors, from the Graeco-Bactrian kingdom, from the Central-Asian invaders, and finally even from the Muhammadans. This is probably the reason why, in a small collection of Lap-cha tales, so many familiar motives and themes can be noticed that are common to the folk-lores of European and other nations.

It would be better therefore, to mention the most typical and important motives only—those which bear traces of having been composed to suit the local surroundings. The most interesting of these is undoubtedly the Lap-cha hero.

The birth of a hero or merely the hero's animal is attributed to the swallowing of a hail-stone (XXVI, 2; XXVIII, 2). The heroes are born in some particular way (XXVI, 3; XXVIII, 2); or as twins (XXIV, 5); and almost invariably they are exposed in some way to the danger of destruction, they are buried or thrown away, etc. In some cases the *Rum* or the parents watch the fate of the child from Heaven and make plans to save him (XXVI, 3; XXVIII, 2). Or this is done through a bitch (XXIV, 11); and two peasants, a 'Grandfather and a Grandmother' bring them up.

The hero's equipment, like those of many European tales, is a magic sword, a golden hat (helmet?), an invisible hat, and a bow and arrow. Sometimes (XXVIII, 6) magical arrows are used, also other enchanted implements, such as a rope and stick (XXIV, 17). On one occasion a sling is mentioned (XXIV, 15).

The hero's mount is always a horse (although he is known in many cases to have walked). These horses are as wonderful as their masters, and must have originally belonged to the solar myth (XXV; XXVI).

The hero starts his career very early, when he is but a child, and according to the *Rong* custom, is still feeding at his mother's breast. If not a re-incarnated *Rum*, he invariably appears as an orphan boy.

Marriages of the hero are related in the style which characterizes the Lap-cha looseness. Most of them return from their adventures with a considerable collection of wives (XXVI; XXVII). Surplus wives may be presented to a friend of the husband (XXVI, 12). They are sometimes the object of gambling (XXI). In the case of the prolonged absence of the husband, the wife may be sold by relatives as 'unclaimed property' (XXVIII, 5).

The adventures of the hero are usually undertaken as the

result of obeying the orders of a king, who is ill-advised by some intriguing individual, who has a demoniacal character. All the exploits are of a fantastic nature, and very rarely is there a note of reality. It is not courage or bravery but cunning and plotting that bring success to the hero, and his magical powers bring him tremendous luck.

'Helpful Animals' are not so prominent here as is usually common in folk-lore, though they are mentioned in the zoological myths (XIV; XX; XXI; XXII). Instead of this help however, the hero always has at his disposal animals with magical powers. This motive is often repeated in the stories of the decisive gambling of animals, in cock-fights, and is also mentioned in the contests of other quadrupeds (XXI; XXVI). Demons are not only partial to this, but arrange it on a larger and more elaborate scale (XXVI). The metamorphosis of a hero is not mentioned frequently; once only we are told that *Ling-gyaso* turns into a flea (XXVIII).

The supernatural beings assisting the heroes are chiefly fairies, the wives or the sisters of demons, serpents, or ogres, etc. They reveal the hiding place of the external soul of their husband or brother (XXV; XXVI; XXVIII) or give generally useful information. Sometimes the helpful being is also a demon (XXVI).

The hero of a tale never becomes wounded or sick, though he is killed falling from a height. Thus dies one of the twin-heroes, after marvellous flights through the skies. One of them is also killed on another occasion when he is wrestliug with his brother on the roof. Or the hero may be dismembered by a magic process (XXVII). In both cases he is resuscitated either by magic yaks' tails that are black and white, or by waters that are of the same colour (XXIV; XXVII). But his normal ending—so to say—is ascension into Heaven where he flies up with all his family, and favourite animals (XXVI). There is never any mention of a burial.

It is strange that the hero is always moving about alone—we never hear of a crowd of admiring followers or attendants. There is instead, only the figure of a 'king,' a ruler who cooks his own dinner (XXIV), and who gambles with his subjects for a wife, and there are only occasional vague mentions of court-servants and advisers.

These are the features of the heroic tales, other stories follow these details, though the object to be reached is different. An element of fun is present, not only in the animal stories (which are told simply to create amusement) but also in the tales about a fool or a liar (XXIX; XXX).

As purely humorous are the stories about the tricks of the jackal (XIII); the bat evading taxes (XVI); and the adventures of a flea (XVIII). Others have apparently a moral inclination, like the tale of the cat with the rats (XVII). The majority are reflections of a mythological nature however, and have been discussed above.

In the stories in which not only animals are actors, but also humans and demons, there are many familiar motives: the story of the crab (XIX), a parallel of 'Puss in Boots' in the form of a squirrel (XX), the tale of a fairy disguised as a black puppy by night, and resuming her form of a maiden by day (XXI), which probably gives the meaning of the solar cycle.

Variants of the same motive appear in the next two tales (XXII; XXIII); in which a maiden comes out of the sacrificial sheepskin which is given to an orphan boy as alms, and in the other a king is disguised as a goat's tail.

Other motives that may be mentioned are the following:—(1) the version of the familiar story about a step-daughter who is depressed by her step-mother (XXXV); (2) the details of a tree on which the hearts of the dead are hanging, and which resembles the Muhammadan idea of the tree of predestination (XXXV).

It is indeed strange to notice how similar in detail is the creative power of man's imagination, and how identical the motives of popular tales may be that are told in the Himalayas, to those that are repeated in western countries thousands of miles away.

3. Tales.

A. Myths of Creation.

I. The Story of Creation.
(1) The children of *It-mo*, (2) The children of *Na-zong-nyo*, (3) *Takbo-thing* and *Na-zong-nyo* descend upon the earth, (4) *Takbo-thing* and *Na-zong-nyo* expelled. (5) The separation of the pair. (6) *Na-zong-nyo* pursues *Takbo-thing*. (7) *Na-zong-nyo* gives to a human being. (8) Miscarried message of immortality. (9) *Na-zong-nyo* finds *Takbo-thing*, but is rejected by him. (10) The sky is ornamented. (11) The Creator sends a *Bong-thing* (12) The covenant with the *Mung*. (13) The first man *Tarbong-mu*. (14) *Narib-nom's* kinsmen interfere. (15) The story of the '*chi*' ferment. (16) The *Matli-mu's* revenge. (17) The *pa-vin-bu* snake tries drinking '*chi*.' (18) The *Rum's* decision.

II. The Birth of the Cloud-demon.

III. The death of the Cloud-demon.

IV. The first Man and the first Sacrifice.
(1) The first man. (2) The first sacrifice. (3) The revolt of the parts of *Tashey-thing's* body.

V. The Progenitor of the Lap-chas.

VI. The Flood and the Serpent-king.

VII. The Flood and the Great Tower.
(1) The flood. (2) The tower.

I. The Story of Creation.

(Told by Toonget Sharap Dorje. a lama, at the Ling-them monastery, who through illness was unable to finish it. May 8th–May 12th.)

1. *The children of It-mo.*

In the beginning the *Himalayas* were created, and two of these mountains, the *Tang-sheng* and the *Narem* were husband and wife. The *Anden-chu* is their son, for he is a snow mountain, and lying at his feet just below, is a table-land called the *Sabur-ancho* where the first man and woman lived. (A great many of the Rong-folk who are derived from that place call themselves *Sabur* to this day.)

The Himalaya mountains are the elder brother and sister to every other land and river afterwards created, the next brother lives in the *Rum-lyang.*[1] He has only one eye, he watches over everybody and holds a pair of scales in his hands with which he weighs their balance.[2]

The next elder sister is called the *Fyong-talyada.* She is a lake lying in the mountains at the source of the *Marmu* river that runs into the *Rung-nyo*[3] at *Dikchu.* She is over three miles in length, and her colours are black, white and red. She can be seen five miles away, but no one has ever been there—for there is no path.

Next to her comes a son, he is the Spirit of the Earthquake (the Mut-li-tyu), his mouth is very very long. He lives in the world below the earth where there is a great wind. Above that there is a region of fire, and above that again an expanse of water which supports the earth. When anything great in this world occurs, be it good or evil, he is known to move.

Next to him comes a daughter, a lake called *Laksom* near *Tassiding*, and below this in the *Bhutan* territory is another son, he is the mountain called *Miduk-cho.* Below him again there is a lake in the Himalayas who is a sister, and her name is *Charla.* But these are only some of the brothers and sisters for all of *It-mo's*[4] children could never be given.

---

[1] *Folk-lore of the Rong-folk.* I also heard another story about the *Rum-lyang*, the country of the gods, which runs as follows :—The *Rum* country is flower-like, the people inhabit the calyx during life (*rid-adek*), while it is on the petals that heaven lies. Time is so long on earth, that a hundred months of our time equals one day. Everyone is good there on the petals, drink is equal to '*chi u-rok*,' the Spirit of '*chi*.' (When this drink runs down to earth, it becomes water, and when it goes down still lower to Hell (*a-mok*) it turns into poison (*ma-ro rip sak*). The people in that place, we are told, lack water, the country is wretched and sorrowful, and when they spit their spittle is licked up by those who are within reach and very thirsty.

[2] In none of the other tales is there any mention of this 'Angel of Fate,' and therefore more detailed characteristics cannot be obtained.

[3] The *Rung-nyo ung* is now known under its Hindu name as the *Tista* river.

[4] See above, p. 337

2. *The children of Nazong-ngyu.*

The two last to be born were *Takbo-thing* and *Nazong-ngyu*, and although these were brother and sister, they became husband and wife and had many children.

The first was the Evil Spirit of Small-pox (*rum-du-mung* and *rurn-du*), the second was the Evil Spirit of Leprosy (*dom mung*), the third was the Evil Spirit of misfortune (*arot-mung*), while the fourth was the Evil Spirit causing mothers to die in child-birth, and is also the Evil Spirit causing the death of unborn children (*asor-mung*). The fifth was the Evil Spirit of Hate and Discord (*mik-jit*), whilst after this many snakes were born (*bu*), among them being the black snake that is not poisonous (*pa-mol-bu*) and many cobras (*pa-hryuk-bu*).

Nazong-ngyu hid all these births, and threw them away without feeding them from her breast. Later, lizards (*sa-mung*) were born, also the smaller kind of lizard (*ta-glot*) and many kinds of different caterpillars (*tun-nyom*), but these were also thrown away.

3. *Takbo-thing and Nazong-ngyu descend upon the earth.*

Then *Takbo-thing* and *Nazong-ngyu* came down to the earth and reached the tableland of *Tarkol-partam* (and this can be seen on clear days from *Ling-them*). When it became night, and they went to sleep, *Nazong-ngyu* took off her bracelet which was called *Pandur* as it was hurting *Takbo-thing's* neck, and placed it on the pillow by her side. The next morning they found it had grown into a tall sago-palm (*sa-nyol-kun*), and it was so high that it reached the sky.[1]

4. *Takbo-thing and Na-zong-ngyu expelled.*

Now when these children grew up the *Rum* country heard about them, and finding *Nazong-ngyu* had given birth to a great many children, they asked her who the father was. This, however she would not divulge.

The *Rum* then decided they would give a reward to anyone who would tell them who the father of *Nazong-ngyu's* children was, but for a long time no one ventured.

At last the dog spoke who lay on her doorstep :—" If you give me the reward I want," he said to the *Rum*, " I will tell you who the father of the children is." The *Rum* asked the dog what he wanted, and he replied that he wanted all the scraps of food he could get from human beings. To this request they agreed and the dog said :—" I am *Nazong-ngyu's* door-keeper and

---

[1] More about this mythical tree, which apparently is nothing but the Cloud tree in the mythology of many nations, is given later. See tales No II and III.

saw *Takbo-thing* go in to her, he stepped over me, and it is he who is the father of all these creatures." [1]

As he was speaking, *Nazong-ngyu*, who was spinning cotton became angry with the dog, and cursing, threw the ball of thread at him and hit him. Then the *Rum* told *Takbo-thing* and *Nazong-ngyu* they had done great wrong and would have to separate.

5. *The separation of the divine pair.*

When these two parted, they divided all their goods, their gold and their silver, *Takbo-thing* putting all his in many bags, but *Nazong-ngyu* hid all hers in the folds of her dress (*dum-pin*).[2] As for the cattle, *Takbo-thing* tied all his up, but *Nazong-ngyu* let hers loose. The fowls they also divided, *Takbo-thing* put his in safe places, in *Yahar*, the white plain towards India, in *Gyanock* the black plain towards China, and in the *Pot-lyang* which is Tibet.[3] But *Nazong-ngyu* let all hers loose and they flew into the jungle. (That is why all the neighbouring countries are so rich and why this country is so poor—some animals are found in the jungle, but they all are *Nazong-ngyu's* which she let loose.)

6. *Nazong-ngyu pursues Takbo thing.*

Now after parting from *Nazong-ngyu*, *Takbo-thing* ran away and made his Palace in the Peacock Mountain. (This is a snow-peak and can be seen from Ling-them on a clear day.)

Nazong-ngyu followed him but could not climb to the top of the high mountain where he lived, so she became very sorrowful and wept bitterly. Giving up any hope of ever meeting him, she cut off one of her plaits of hair and threw it to the top of the mountain.[4]

After that, she called her children, the grasshoppers including all the locusts, and told them she was going to build a stair-case with her necklaces in order to reach the top of the mountain, and that they were to hold on to it firmly.

---

[1] Should *Takbo-thing* be in reality a lunar deity, the betrayal by the dog is quite a typical part of the myth—dogs are known to bark and howl at the sight of the moon. Cf. A. de Gubernatis, *Zoological Mythology*, London, 1872, vol. ii, p. 19 (footnote).

[2] The end a Lap-cha woman makes in her cloth dress and tucks into her waist.

[3] All these safe countries, extending in all directions from Sikhim, are obviously nothing but the sky, and the herd, or stars, themselves. The symbolism of the moon being a shepherd of the Celestial herd is quite common in folk-lore.

[4] The Lap-cha woman used formerly to cut off one of her plaits when she became a widow (usually they have two). The symbolism of this story probably alludes to the first ray of the morning sun catching the high peaks of the mountain.

I have also heard it mentioned that when a wife committed adultery formerly, for a punishment she had her nose cut off and one of her plaits.

But most of them became greedy, and wanted to steal their mother's precious stones, and they forgot their promise to her and went away with as much as they could carry. But two did not run away, these two were daddy-long-legs, *Namgel* and *Ma-un-gnyu*, who never left the stair-case. (This is the reason why all grasshoppers die within three months, they are still punished and have to die; it is the daddy-long-legs who is the only insect who lives for a long time, in fact they only die when man kills them, and their legs grew to the enormous length they now are owing to the fact that they had to hold on so long to the stair-case.)[1]

7. *Nazong-ngyu gives birth to a Human Being.*

When *Nazong-ngyu* almost reached the top of the mountain, she gave birth to a human being, a son whom she loved and fed from her breast. Her other children seeing this became jealous, and through their hatred and jealousy the child died.

So *Nazong-ngyu* built two tombs, one was called *Re-bu* and was meant for a *Mung*, while the other was called *Sheng-bu* and was meant for a *Rum*.[2]

8. *Miscarried Message of Immortality.*

Then she sent two birds, the *rakchum-fo* and the *ran-fon-fo* up to *Takbo-thing* to fetch the two waters, the one that gives life, and the one that takes it.[3] He asked the two messengers what they had come for and they replied :—"*Nazong-ngyu* has borne you a son in the world, but he has died and she sent us to fetch the two waters."

Takbo-thing gave them to the two birds and instructed them to pour the one that gave life over the *Rum's* tomb, while the one that took life they were to pour over the *Mung's* tomb.

As the two birds were flying back to *Nazong-ngyu*, they talked this over, and thought if they obeyed *Takbo-thing's* directions the *Rum* would have only one life—he would never die to be re-incarnated while if they gave the water that took life to the *Mung*, he would die to be re-incarnated and would increase and fill the world.

So when the two messengers came down from the sky and alighted, they poured the water that took life over the *Rum's*

---

1 The idea underlying the treacherous behaviour of the grasshoppers and the locusts is apparently an allusion to the hiding of these insects with the arrival of dawn.

2 The symbolism of these two tombs is not clear. Nothing is said about the appearance of the *Mung*, perhaps these two were twins ?

3 For references to the water of life and water of death, see further on tale No. XXVII. These liquids are said to be of a black and white colour. Cf. J. Frazer, *The Golden Bough*, xi, pp. 114-115.

tomb, while the one that gave life they poured over the *Mung's* tomb. So it happened the *Rum's* life would never be endless, he would die to be born again, and he would increase and fill the world, whilst the *Mung* would only live once.[1]

9. *Nazong-ngyu finds Takbo-thing, but is rejected by him.*

After this *Nazong-ngyu* went up still further and nearly reached *Takbo-thing*, only he refused to see her, and she built a separate palace to live in. (This palace can still be seen from *Ling-them* on a clear day, and we the Rong-folk believe *Takbo-thing* and *Nazong-ngyu* still live there, and we offer them sacrifices, for were they not our first father and mother ?)

10. *The Sky is ornamented.*

This was the commencement of creation, but the sky was quite empty for there was no sun or moon, it was only blue and had no ornaments, so the Creator decorated it with many stars. Still the sky did not show all its beauty, and the Creator ornamented it with clouds so that the mountains were sometimes shaded, and he saw it was good.

11. *The Creator sends a Bong-thing.*

Everything was nearly completed, but a *Bong-thing* was required as a mediator to speak between the *Rum* and the Humans.[2]

So from Heaven (the *Rum-lyang*) *It-mo*, the Creator sent a bamboo (the *prong*), but he only went to the top of a mountain where he planted himself and spread and did not do the work of a go-between.

Then a beetle (the *tang-dare*) was sent, but he too neglected the work of a go-between, and only planted a species of mimosa (the *sus-gryonkun*).[3]

So the Creator sent another beetle (the *la-gyok*), but he also started planting a species of Batula (the *sus-li-kun*) and a

---

[1] For the parallels to this story of the miscarried message of immortality, see J. Frazer, *Folklore of the Old Testament*, vol. I, pp. 47–52.

[2] The *Bong-thing* is nowadays a sort of *shaman*, i.e. a medicine man, an exorciser who cures the sick. Details of his office were given me by *Pasang*, a *Bong-thing* at *Badamtam*, who had counted his beads to know whether it would be propitious coming to see me or not. Nov. 13th. When a man is sick he first burns incense to know whether it is the *Rum* or the *Mung* who are troubling the patient. By counting his beads, chanting from a book, and throwing dice, he finds out what is to be done. Then he falls into a trance, and speaks the words that rise to his lips whilst he continues to burn incense.

[3] Divine mission and special sacredness are attributed to different kinds of beetles in most folk-lore, cf. Gubernatis, op. cit., vol. ii, pp. 195, 209.

tree called the *sus-lok-kun*, and he was of no use as a go-between (He is the beetle who sings "*trem-trem-yeng-yeng*" or just "*yeng-yeng-yeng*" every night during the fourth month of the year till the eighth month, by the Tibetan calendar, and then he dies).

Then the Creator sent a grasshopper[1] (the *thenum-jit-nyom*). He came and planted the bamboo called the *mat-lo* from which arrows and darts are made, and also the elephant grass that grew later with *Tashey-thing's* pony's teeth-marks on them.[2]

So he was of no use, and the Creator sent a black cricket (the *num-brit*). He cries loudly like this at night—*ti-re-re-re*, but he did no work and only kept going in and out of holes all night.

Then there was only one child of the Creator's left, and he didn't wish to leave home (*li*), but the Creator who loved him like a mother told him he ought to go and see his brothers and sisters, the Himalaya Mountains, the lakes and all the rivers in order that he might become a *Bong-thing* to help the humans with the evil spirits.

And the child asked *It-mo* what would be the best things to take with him, and the Creator gave him some ginger (*salep*), some garlic (*paki-mun-gu*), and a tree—the fruit of which he could place on a stick and burn slowly like a lamp (the *safi-kun*). And all these things are used externally and internally by the *Bong-thing* to-day, and from all these plants and bulbs medicine is made.

Taking all these bulbs the son came to the *Lung-tan-parten* table-land in the Himalayas, but he found the *Mung* had already come to that place, indeed they had spread over the whole country, they were in all the mountains, in all the trees and in all the caves. So he said to them :—" I was sent to go round the world, but you seem to have been everywhere before me so I will return to the Creator."

12. *The Covenant with the Mung.*

But when he turned and was leaving, the *Mung* caught hold of him saying :—" On one condition we will do everything you command, when we worry the human beings with disease and illness, we will go away and leave them in peace if, in return, you will give us something, fowls, eggs, pigs, or any other animal."

The *Bong-thing* said :—" You force me to do this, only swear

---

[1] The grasshopper's importance is very great in folk-lore. Amongst the African Bushmen he appears as the creator, see Hastings' *Encyclopœdia* vol. i, p. 490.

[2] In story No. XXV, these marks are attributed to the steed of *Gabu*—not to *Tashey-thing's* horse.

you will leave all human beings in peace. I will call my brothers the *Sakbri-bu* and the *Sahnang-bu* to act as witnesses."

To this they all agreed, and at *Partam Sakber* the *Mung* swore that when they worried a human person with illness they would agree to leave the sick person in peace were the *Bong-thing* to attend to the patient, and propitiate them, the *Mung* by giving an offering of a cow, a pig, or several goats.

To make doubly sure, the *Bong-thing* asked the *Mung* to swear by spitting[1] on a rock there which they did, and the oath was so great, it shattered the rock to pieces. And again he asked them to swear and spit in the lake, which they did, but the oath was so great, it caused the lake to dry up. Yet once more he asked them to swear spitting on a tree, which they did, but the tree could not bear the weight of the oath and it fell.

This was the covenant between the *Bong-thing* and the *Mung*, and we the Rong-folk believe this was the origin of the *Bong-thing*.

And the *Bong-thing* was satisfied and planted for us, Rong-folk, the plantain (*tuk-blo*) that bears big fruit, many kinds of bamboo (the *po*), and the yam (*sun-than*), while for the *Lum*, the native in the Plains, he planted the tree-fern, for those in *Bhutan* and *Gya-nok* (China) he planted a species of Amomum (*pa-la*), and for the Tibetan (the *Pat-mo*), he planted the elephant grass (the *pa-shor*).

And when he had done this he went up to Tiamtan where he built a palace, and we the Rong-folk believe he still lives there. It is a country that lies midway between Heaven (the *Rum-lyang*) and earth.[2]

13. *The First Man, Tarbong-mu.*

After the *Bong-thing* another son was born to the Creator, *Tarbong-mu*, and the child, after sucking the breast, wished to see his brothers and sisters and came up to this world.

He arrived first of all at the *Minduk Cho*, his snow-mountain brother in *Bhutan*, and from there he went to see his elder sister, the *Charla* lake. Then he went to see his elder brother, the *Kang-chhen* mountain, and from that "highest curtain of snow" he looked well all round, but could see nothing. At last he looked towards the *Dinzyong-lyang*, and saw in the middle of the table-land a tree (*pu-lil sumpyer*) bearing many kinds of fruit. It had a great many birds sitting on its branches, the *kal-het* was there, the *ka-dong*, the pheasant, the

---

[1] Spitting in water and swearing on a stone and a tree are still common in Sikhim. It is common among various primitive races, cf. Hastings' *Encyclopœdia*, vol. 4, p. 208. A similar oath is described in the stories of Nos. XX, 2; XXVI, 8.

[2] Cf. above, p. 337. Also called *Sari-rung* or *Siri-nong-dong-chen*.

blue-horned pheasant, the great barbet, another kind of pheasant and many others.

Tarbong-mu thought he would catch all these birds and give them to his mother as a present. So he wove a net from a creeper (*ta-kli*) and caught a great many. These he carried down to his mother who was very pleased, and as she wished for some more he came up once more to the world.

The following day he went to see how many birds he had caught, but to his surprise he only found pieces of wood, and watching, discovered that a fairy from the *Rum* country had been placing them there. She was so beautiful that her beauty cannot be described, her name was *Narib-nom*, the daughter of *Lha-mayen*. He told his mother that he had fallen in love with her and would come up to the world to try and catch her. When he saw her the next day at sunrise, he darted upon her and caught her. They struggled and came to the *Sa-ryum* mountains, there he defeated her and making her his wife, she became fruitful.

14. *Narib-nom's kinsmen interfere.*

This fact came to the notice of the *Rum* brothers who met and consulted, but they could not decide what they should do to *Tarbong-mu* and *Narib-nom*. They were so uncertain that they prepared to make '*chi*,' and to think it over whilst they sipped it. They had the millet but no ferment.

15. *The story of the 'chi' ferment.*

Then the wasp who lives in a mud nest (*ta-lyam*) told the *Rum* if they would give him a present, he would find out *Mat-li-mu's* abode and fetch it for them. What he wanted were the remains of the butter in the closely-woven basket that was kept for that purpose (*mor tok*), and the *Rum* promised him this. (Ever since that day the basket should always be kept in a safe place, else that wasp will make a hole and take his share.)

So he went down to the *Mat-li-mu's* land which was below the earth, and found she was a very old woman. He lived with her as her grandson, and fetched and carried for her, and worked so hard that at last she grew to love him.

Once she even made '*chi*' from some millet, but at the time of putting in the ferment, she covered the wasp up in a closely-woven basket (*tun-gar*). He cried out at once loudly that were she to cover him up like that he would be able to see the whole world including herself. The old woman asked him what she should cover him with in order to make him blind, and he told her to place him in a big basket with a wide mesh (*tun-dyon*). Believing him, the old woman put him inside one, and he saw her take the ferment from the nape of her neck which she put in the '*chi.*' Then he asked to be taken out quickly as he was suffocating.

Later one day he asked if he might hunt for lice in her hair, and as he searched, the old woman fell asleep. The wasp took the ferment from her neck, and flew back to the world of the humans again.

16. *The Mat-li-mu's revenge.*

He had nearly reached there when the old woman woke and cried out :—" You have stolen my ferment, if you only know how to use it, you would be able to offer the '*chi*' to the *Rum*, but now you will find that it always excites you, it will cause you all to quarrel, it may, even perhaps, kill you."

But the wasp started to make '*chi*' as he had brought the ferment back, and all the *Rum* came, but no one dared taste it, as they did not know what would happen to the first one who drank.

17. *The pa-vin-bu snake tries drinking* '*chi.*'

Then the *pa-vin-bu* volunteered to try it first (and he is the snake who springs from trees). As soon as he had drunk a little, he became mad, and commenced to fly, and some of his friends went to look after him. They found, however, he was not dying, and another snake—one that is black, the *pa-mol-bu*, drank, also became mad. He went into a cave, and some of his friends went in too to look after him, but they found he was only snoring.

Then a third snake—one that is poisonous, the *pa-hlyok-bu*, volunteered. He drank the '*chi*', and went away vomiting, and ever since that day he is more poisonous.

Then a fourth offered to taste it—the hornet that has a red head and a black body (*tik*). She had some and only ran away drunk.

After that came another snake—the *pa-zyob-bu* who only lives in the hills—and when he had gone everyone thought they might try as the poison had by now all gone.

18. *The Rum's Decision.*

And the *Rum* came to the conclusion that *Tarbong-mu* and *Narib-nom* ought to be married, and the fairy started cultivating millet in order to celebrate the wedding, whilst *Tarbong-mu* went up to *Tibet* (*Pot-lyang*) to fetch silk, cloth, and many valuable clothes. On his return he visited the Plains (*Tin--lyang*), so that he could fetch a pig, and it was then that *Narib-nom* cut the millet. They killed the pig, put on the new clothes, and the wedding ceremony commenced.

This is the origin of '*chi*' and how it came to be used by the *Rong*-folk.[1]

II. The Birth of the Cloud-demon.

(*Told by Shupa at Lang-dang, May 6th.*)

In the beginning the father *Pa-sandi* and the Creator-mother *It-mo* had a son and daughter who were called *Takbo-thing* and *Na-zong-ngyu.*

Takbo-thing slept on the *Naho-da* lake while his sister was on the *Nathar* lake. Now one day she made a golden staircase from her lake to her brother's, and thus he was tempted, came one night to his sister and slept with her.

During the night the bracelet she was wearing hurt her brother's neck, so she took it off and placed it beside her pillow. The next morning it had grown up into a sago palm tree (*sa-nyol-kun*).[2] Later it flowered, and the flowers became snow and hailstones when they fell on the earth.

Then *Na-zong-ngyu* gave birth to a son who was called the *Laso-mung pono.* He lived on the top of the sago palm and his after-birth was known as the *Mara-mung.*[3] If you care to see them, you must climb the hill and look at the *Sa-nyol* mountain where you will see a big opening at the foot of the petrified trunk where the *Mara-mung* is hiding. He flies about at night sometimes looking like fire.

III. The Death of the Cloud-demon and the Origin of Kings.

(*Told by Apon at Pakhyang, April 28th.*)

Now in Sikhim, a country lying in the Himalaya mountains, there was a big tree called the sago palm (*sa-nyol*). The demon *Laso-mung-pono* used to live on it, and he gave so much trouble to the people of the *Densyong-lyang* that they decided to cut down the tree.

---

1 '*Chi*' is the local intoxicating drink. It is made from the millet plant, whose nutritious seeds are dried in the sun for three days when they are ripe. Three compressors are used. The seed is first boiled in an earthenware pot which is covered with a loose bamboo mat (the *tang-gryon-fuk*) which is covered by another larger vessel. Over that another pot is placed round which plantain bark and mud is wrapped. The large pot is filled with water and dropped into the small pot. When the seeds have fermented but little, and the drink is sweet, it is much sought after by women; it is after several days' exposure to the sun when the grain has thoroughly fermented that it becomes very strong.

2 The sago-palm tree is frequently seen in Sikhim and in Bengal. It is said to attract flies greatly, and for this reason people are said to cut it down when found in their compounds.

3 Cf. the belief of the Baganda who regard the after-birth as a twin of the child; it is buried under a tree and regarded as a ghost. See Hastings' *Encyclopædia*, vol. xii, p. 500, who also quotes Roscoe, *Baganda*, pp. 52, 54.

When they had cut it down, the demon flew away. A gush of water came out from the spot the tree had stood on, becoming the source of the *Rung-nyo-ung* or the *Tista* river. The demon, however, kept following the people, and sat on the *singli-sang-lok*[1] tree which was crushed by his weight. Then he moved to the *sichem*[2] tree, which although small, bore his weight.

There the people shot at him with their bows and arrows, and at last slashed at him with their knives (*ban*).

Those who came and stood near him as he was dying were the *Aden-mu* (the *Adinpuso* ?) a family of kings. As he was breathing his last, a family called the *Luksom-mo,* second only to the family of kings stood near him, later came the family of *Sanut-mung.* More than a hundred families helped to cut him up, and out of his pieces of flesh many kinds of wasps sprang up, some of them being the hornet (*tik*), the yellow wasp (*ta-lyo*), the *ta-lyam*, another species of wasp and the *sum-myar* a large wasp, with many kinds of the common black fly like the *sum-bryong.* The demon's bones were thrown into the air becoming mosquitoes (*sait*).[3]

IV. The First Man and the First Sacrifice.

(*Chanted by Karma Csyodek at Dickhu, April 25th.*)

1. *The First Man.*

In the beginning there was only sea, and the Creator, *Tashey-takbo-thing*, made two kinds of fish, *ngo* was the common kind, while the *ngo-yang* had a serpent form.

From the sea we believe that a tortoise supports the world, and on it *Tashey-takbo-thing* created the birds and animals.[4]

Then he tried to make a form of man from butter, but it would not stand up, as whenever he made it, it melted. (Had the butter only remained firm, we should all have been very beautiful).[5]

Then he made a human form of earth and mud, and wind came into this resemblance of man and life was created. Then *Tashey-takbo-thing* made blood out of water which he put in it,

---

[1] This is a big tree, very tall, that grows in tropical countries.

[2] This is a tree growing in tropical countries near water, a species of elm.

[3] This is an interesting parallel to the ancient idea that the origin of bees is from a dismembered solar or lunar deity, as in the myths of Dionysus or in the Biblical legend of *Samson and his lion,* cf. Gubernatis, op. cit., vol. ii, pp. 217-218.

[4] This is a story that is similar to one told by the *Santals* of Bengal in a much more detailed form. See J. Frazer, *Folk-lore in the Old Testament,* vol. i, pp. 19–22.

[5] The different conceptions arising about the creation of man have been admirably summed up in J. Frazer's *Folk-lore in the Old Testament,* vol. i, pp. 3–44 (as quoted).

and the bones he created from stone. Then he moved away to see whether the creature he had made could answer him, and speak, but as he had no veins or nerves he was unable to. So *Tashey-takbo-thing* picked a great many creepers from the jungle and from these which he spread all over the form it spoke.

Thus was the first male created, but as there was no female, he was lonely, and could not reproduce himself.

One day as he was catching birds with his snare in the jungle, *Tashey-takbo-thing* entangled a woman in one for him to catch.

So the man caught her, and took her to his home, but at first they could not marry as there was no go-between to help them talk over the marriage matters. But at last the *Rum* decided to send the owl (*tam-bun*) down to the Country of Creation (*It-lyang*).

2. *The First Sacrifice.*

Then *Tashey-takbo-thing* wished to make his first sacrifice to the *Rum*, and called the *gno* and the *ngo-yong*. These two argued who should go, and decided at last it should be the one who was able to jump over the water-fall. *Gno* tried, but failed as he was dragged under by the water. *Gno-yong* however, succeeded and that is how we Rong-folk know that they can go up all rivers while the *gno* have to stay in the Plains.

3. *The Revolt of the Parts of Tashey-takbo-thing's Body.*

At the offering time the hands and feet of *Tashey-takbo-thing* quarrelled with his belly saying :—"We work very hard the whole time, but you, the belly, do nothing." And the belly replying said :—"Very well then, as you believe that, for two or three days I shall do really nothing. I will rest and shall not eat anything."

Then the hands and feet became so weak they could do nothing, and were soon unable to move. And the belly said :—"If you find me something to eat, you will find you regain strength and vigour," and as he ate a little, the hands and feet planted strength and they knew they were defeated. So they regained sugar-cane, (*mut pa-am*) pine-apples (*bor-pot*) and all kinds of fruit which grew abundantly.[1]

And *Tashey-takbo-thing* took a supply of all these fruits with many fish from the rivers and sacrificed them. This was the commencement of all offering. It took place a long time before Buddhism was introduced into his country, and even now, we

---

[1] The rebellion of parts of *Tashey-takbo-thing*'s body has probably been introduced into this tale of the first sacrifice by mistake—it has no logical connection with it.

the *Rong-folk*, hold sacrifices twice a year at the harvest and sowing times.[1]

V. The Progenitor of the Lap-chas.

(Told by Topden of Panang at Ling-them, May 8th.)

At the foot of the *Himalaya* mountains there lies a lake called the *Rimband*, and a rock the *Kong-lahab* hangs over it.

In the beginning the fairy of the lake made that rock her loom and wove. Whilst she was weaving, one of the *Rum* gods looked down and saw her and desired her. He turned himself into a monkey, and coming down to that lake he made her his wife.[2]

A son was born to them whom they called *Sangel*, and when he was older he also married a fairy of that lake.

And we the Rong-folk believe we are descended from him.[3] For we still offer sacrifices on that rock in the month when we harvest the rice. Every year we give fish (*gno*), game (*fo*),

---

[1] The *Rong*-folk have told me in many different villages, including those of *Lang-dang, Ling-them, Kabi*, etc., that they hold sacrifices twice a year, at harvest and sowing time to ensure good crops, and that the Maharaja also holds them. The first ceremony takes place in September, while the second, which commences on the 13th of December, I had the honour of attending in the Palace grounds at Gjangtok, through the kindness of H.H. Sir Tashe Namgyal, the Maharaja of Sikhim. Both ceremonies illustrate stories that are sung to the accompaniment of a lamas' dance. The first one is a celebration of the War-dance, and is held to 'celebrate the Worship of the Spirit of the *Kangchen-Dzod-Nga* (*Kinchinjunga*, the *Rong*-folk name being the *Kong-chin-chu*), who is shortly called *Dzod-nga*, meaning the five treasures. He is believed to be the God *Kuvera* (*rNam-sras-mDung-dMar-chah Kuvera* with the red spear). He is represented as the War-God in Sikhim, and has to be worshipped periodically. He is believed to belong to that class of spirit called *Yakashas* by the Hindus (*Tib-gNop-sByins*). In this ceremony the sacrifice to the Spirit of the *Kong-chin-chu* group seems to have changed to a War-dance instituted as 'a physical exercise to counteract the effects of the sedentary life of the lamas.' The second ceremony that is now held was originally the Lamas' 'devil dancing cult for exorcising malignant and human enemies. The lamas altered the motive of the play to hang upon it their own sacerdotal story for their own glorification and priestly gain.' This will show how Buddhism is sweeping away the old Lap-cha religion. I hold the translated descriptions of both ceremonies.

[2] Cf. other parallels of the monkey being the progenitor of mankind. See J. Frazer, *Folk-lore in the Old Testament*, vol. i, p. 35. This myth recalls in some degree the well-known Hindu tales of the *Ramayana*, concerning Sita and Hanuman. The northern equivalent of the monkey, the bear, is often connected in folk-lore of different European nations, with the motive of marrying a human wife who gives birth to a half-man and half-bear. *Cf.* Gubernatis, *op. cit.*, vol. ii, pp. 116–118.

[3] The only story I heard from a Lap-cha of monkeys being degenerated men was from the *Achen mandál* at Lopchu (Bengal). He told me that some of the Rong-folk believed that once upon a time a man started making a shelf for a fire-place (*pang-tok*), but cutting the wood he became angry, and running into the wood, the handle of the knife became his tail and he turned into a monkey.

rice-*chi* (*mor-chi*), beaten rice (*ta-la*), and ginger (*himg*). These are put on banana leaves and are offered at *Shara* near the *Tulung* monastery.

VI. The Flood and the Serpent-King.

(*Told by Topden of Panang at Ling-them, May 8th.*)

In the beginning, the world was all water, and there were no living creatures. Then the Creator made an earthenware pot that floated on the water, and this was land that floated on the sea. Like a human body that is made of flesh and bone the earth is made of rock and soil.

In the lowlands the Creator planted the bamboo, and the *sisin-nambyong*. After that he made the *Lang-chuk Lung-dal* that are now known as the Himalaya Mountains, and he created the *pa-song pumun* bamboo which grows at the foot of these hills. And then he created *Pudung-thing* and *Nazong-gnyu* who were the first male and female, and it is from these two that the human-beings have spread over the entire world. Then there was neither birth nor death, but this was created later to suit the world.

The seeds of all these crops were given by *Pudung-thing* and *Nazong-gnyu* to all their children who cultivated the land and lived on the production.

When these two were made, birth so multiplied that there was not enough room in the world. Then *Paril-bu*, who was the Serpent-King dammed the rivers by lying in them, and they overflowed and rose to a great height and reached the sky.[1] Everyone fled to the top of *Kong-chen-chu*, the highest peak in the Himalayas, but only two people were saved. The place where they stood is called *Mayak-kyong* to this day. While the flood was raging, *Tashey-thing* sent a hero down into the world called the *Yong-li-pono* to kill the serpent who was blocking the rivers. The hero cut the serpent in pieces, thus making the waters run down into the Plains, and we, the Rong-folk believe the Blue Mountains (that can be seen from the valley of the *Rangpo Chu*) are the remains of the cut body of the serpent.[2]

---

1 It is characteristic here to note the idea of the serpent causing the flood by damming the rivers. We see in the folk-lore of many nations, and in the *Avesta* and Hindu mythology, that the serpent was very prominent in the act of stopping waters, and to get rid of him a deity or hero is sent to kill him. The Rong-folk believe the *Paril-bu* lives in the *Kong-chin-chu* and that he descends from the mountain fastnesses to cause rain. He is said to be of gigantic proportions and to have a red crest. See Gubernatis, vol. ii, pp. 390–395.

2 Apparently the serpent of gigantic stature is referred to in the story of *Ati-azyak*'s adventures (No. XIX) where we are told of the killing of a monster, although it is not in connection with the flood (stopping the waters is mentioned in the same story however, but connected with another demon). The story of the great flood as it is given in the folk-lore of

When the world was dry once more, *Tashey-thing* sent down two rivers from the Himalaya Mountains guided by a Serpent-King called the *Paril Patong*, and a quail, the *Ko-hun-fo*, and these were the *Rung-nyo* and (the *Tista*) and the *Rung-nyit.*

He also sent *Pudung-thing* and *Nazong-gnyu* down to the world from the height of *Mayal Kyong*, giving them the name of *Tikung-tek* and *Nikong-gnal*. These two are the first Grandfather and Grandmother of the Rong-folk. As they had no king, *Tashey-thing* sent them down *Gyabo-chaya-dor-tulku* from *Mayal Kyong*, and he is the Grandfather (ancestor) of the present Maharaja.

VII. The Flood and the Great Tower.

(*Told by David Macdonald at Kalimpong, April 22nd.*)

1. *The Flood.*

In the beginning *Foog-rong* and *Nazong-nyo* lived, our first Grandfather and Grandmother (ancestors). Then the flood came and nearly every human creature perished, only two who ran to the summit of Mount *Tendong-lho* were saved.[1]

Now *Takbo-thing*[2] was the father of *Tashey-thing* who had married the partridge (*ko-hom-fo*), and she put some '*chi*' in a large leaf (*tung-fyum-nyom*) which she offered to her father-in-law, saying if he only would, he could stop the flood. And *Takbo-thing* looking down from the country of the *Rum* saw that the world was flooded, and that his daughter-in-law was praying to him and offering him '*chi*,' and he took up his walking stick (*pa-tung*) and struck the world so that the water sank in. But the partridge spilt some of the '*chi*' on her breast. (The mark can be seen to this day, she is called the *tung-fyum* because of it.) So the world became dry once more, and the trees and bushes commenced to grow again, and the world was re-peopled.

2. *The Tower.*

When the world was full of people once more, some of the *Rong*-folk, a tribe called the *Na-ong* or Ignorant Persons prepared to ascend to the *Rum* country, and they began building a tower of earthen pots. They piled them so high that the *Rum* country was only one pole away. Then the Creator thought they were becoming too eager and zealous and that it was not good for them.

---

different nations is summarised in J. Frazer, *Folk-lore in the Old Testament*, vol. i, pp. 104–361.

[1] The name given by the Rong-folk to their *Mount Ararat* varies in different parts of the country, most probably the original tradition is lost.

[2] If *Takbo-thing* is really a lunar deity in one of his aspects, his causing the flood to cease at the end of the monsoon rains is quite a clear allusion.

So he thought he would create confusion, and make them all speak in different tongues, so that they would misunderstand one another. The man at the top shouted "*Kok vim yang tale*" (*Hand up the pole with the hook*), while the men at the bottom heard the words "*Chek tala*" (*cut it down*). These wondering greatly shouted up to ask the man at the top whether he really meant it. This time they heard the words "*ak, ak*" (*yes, yes*). And they at once cut the tower down, which falling killed many of the *Na-ong*, and those that remained had to separate on account of their not being able to understand one another.

And even to this day, broken earthen pots are found on that plain which is called *Dalon Partan.*[1]

B. Zoological Mythology.

VIII. *Tashey-thing* and his wives.

(1) *Tashey-thing* marries a she-boar, who attempts to kill him. (2) *Tashey-thing* is saved by a monkey. (3) *Tashey-thing* pursues the boar and kills her. (4) He marries a fish.

IX. The Two Suns.

(1) The toad kills one of the two suns. (2) The bat makes the hidden sun smile. (3) The toad punished for killing the sun.

X. The Tiger Hunted by Wind and Lightning.

(1) The wind and lightning search for a wife. (2) They decide to kill the tiger who is the husband of their sister. (3) The tiger is killed and his flesh scattered.

XI. The Tiger and the Toad.

(1) A tiger and a toad lick each other. (2) The tiger, alarmed at the toad, runs away. (3) The toad and the crow.

XII. The Tiger and the Ass.

XIII. The Tiger and the Jackal.

(1) A jackal finds a dead elephant and invites a tiger to share his food. (2) The tiger plots to kill the jackal. (3) The jackal causes the tiger's death. (4) The jackal tries to become a hunter.

XIV. A Jackal tries to Steal a Hen.

XV. The Monkey and the Stork.

XVI. The Bat evades paying Taxes.

XVII. The Cat and the Rats.

(1) Some rats injure a lama's clothes. (2) The lama prays for divine help, and a cat arrives. (3) The rats get killed one by one.

XVIII. The Flea and the Louse.

(1) The flea and the louse go to fetch firewood. (2) The flea hits his wife and calls a priest to cure her. (3) The turtle-dove devours the louse.

---

[1] For parallels to this story—see J. Frazer, *Folk-lore in the Old Testament*, vol. i, pp. 362–387. The present story seems to be substantially the same as the Tibetan (in which the element of the confusion of languages does not appear however). The *Mikirs* also have a version of this. Cf. *Census and Reports of Assam*, 1902, p. 47.

Kumar Polden now owns the plain *Dalon Partan* whom I had the pleasure of meeting at Pakhyong on April 20th.

XIX. A Crab and a Water-wag-tail Hunt a Stag.

(1) A crab and a water-wag-tail kill a stag, but a giant comes and snatches away the body. (2) These two kill the giant's wife. (3) The giant catches the crab who pretends to be dead.

XX. The Services of the Black Squirrel.

(1) The orphan boy spares the life of the squirrel and accepts its servitude. (2) The squirrel procures a Chinese princess as a bride for the orphan boy. (3) The squirrel comes to a cow-shed, and declares it to be the property of his master. (4) They come to the palace of the seven demons, whom the squirrel slays. (5) The orphan boy's sister is brought by the squirrel. (6) The squirrel returns to the *Rum* country.

XXI. A Fairy Disguised as a Puppy.

(1) An orphan boy spares the life of a big fish. (2) He receives a puppy as a reward and brings her home. (3) The king sees the puppy-wife and desires her.

XXII. The Food-producing Skin.

(1) An orphan boy is given the magic skin as charity. (2) A demon attempts to steal the skin. (3) The skin is dropped into the river but recovered.

XXIII. The Last Goat's Tail.

(1) A woman saves the tail of the last goat in the herd. (2) The tail is saved from being cooked by promising its labour. (3) The tail goes to kill bullocks. (4) The tail steals the three bullocks killed by the two princes through a trick. (5) The tail undergoes an ordeal and is ordered to steal guarded treasure. (6) The tail arranges three dances and appears in human form.

VIII. Tashey-thing and his Wives.

(Told by Dang-dang at Rhenock, Sikhim, April 19th.)

1. *Tashey-thing marries Mon-tsu-mot the wild boar who attempts to kill him.*

Once upon a time *Tashey-thing* made friends with *Mon-tsu-mot*, a wild she-boar whom he married, and with whom he lived happily for ten years.

Not far away from their home there was a great rock hanging over a precipice where a rock-bee (*vot*) had its hive, and *Tashey-thing* wished to bring the honey home one day himself.

It was a very dangerous task to reach the rock even with the aid of a rope, and *Tashey-thing* who was being helped by many animals and insects, made them all swear to hold the rope firmly and not to let it go. But his wife *Mon-tsu-mot* was not faithful, and wished to get rid of *Tashey-thing*.

Koeng was one of the beetle rope-holders, for it was the time of year when he lives and sings for three months ; the *bak-dyol* was another beetle who also comes out at this time, whilst the *dyang-dyang* (another beetle) was also alive, so he came too. So did *Neprik-nyom*, the grasshopper and lots of other insects all helped *Tashey-thing* who started climbing down the rope.

But almost immediately *Mon-tsu-mot* cut it, and all the animals and insects became so frightened that they ran away at once.

Tashey-thing saved himself by holding on to the rock by one of the hairs from his moustache—and we *Rong*-folk believe to this day that the leaves from the bush we find hanging down from dry rocks, which has a grey colour like the tint of the thatching grass, and which is soft like hair, originates from the one hair that saved his life.

2. *Tashey-thing is saved by a monkey.*

He was wondering how he would release himself from his peril, when a monkey happened to pass, who asked him what he was doing.

Tashey-thing told him he had come down to take some honey from the rock, but his wife *Mon-tsu-mot* with some animals and insects who had promised to help him, had played a nasty trick, and had cut the rope they had been holding.

So the monkey took him off the rock, and putting him on his back told him he was to keep his eyes closed until he knew by the sound that he, the monkey, was walking; he was on no account to open them especially when they were rustling through leaves.

Now when *Tashey-thing* was put down in a safe place, he told the monkey for a reward he would give him gold, silver or anything he asked for.

But the monkey did not want gold or silver. "Give me" he said "a blessing instead, that will help me to have the first fruits of every field in harvest-time."

And *Tashey-thing* gave him the blessing.

But he cursed the rock-bees, saying much trouble had come to him through them, and that it would be no sin were the Rong-folk to take their honey away in the future.

3. *Tashey-thing pursues the boar and kills her.*

Then *Tashey-thing* planted a species of bamboo (the *bling*) and when it had grown big enough he made a bow from it, and then he planted another bamboo (the *pa-song*) from which he made an arrow. Then for three years he followed the foot-prints of *Mon-su-mot*, and passing through nine countries and crossing nine ranges of mountains, he found the wild boar at last sleeping in a lair she had made of dry leaves. Then he aimed with his arrow, and killing her, he collected firewood and commenced to burn her. Whilst he was roasting her some hot fat fell from her body, and a drop falling on his thumb made him lick it off.

Then he cursed all wild boars, saying it would be no sin henceforth if the Rong-folk were to kill and eat them. So we the Rong-folk believe from that day, we can eat the flesh of the wild boar, which we never did formerly when she was *Tashey-thing's* wife. It was also then that the bow and arrow were invented.

4. *He marries a fish.*

Then being a widower, *Tashey-thing* married *Gnyul-chul* who was a fish, and said once as they came to a river he would carry her across on his back. *Gnyul-chul* did not like the idea, and told *Tashey-thing* he ought to make a bridge. He made a bamboo one and just as they were nearly across, knowing she would annoy him, *Gnyu-chul* tumbled off his back and dropped in.

Then *Tashey-thing* became angry, and running down-stream he placed a bamboo fishing-net (a *yet*), in the middle of the river. Catching her on the third day, he found that the arms and legs of *Gnyu-chul* had become fins, whilst the rest of her body was still that of a woman.

The moment *Tashey-thing* had caught her he made a fire and burnt her. Some fat fell from her body, and dropped on his thumb which he licked off, and he cursed fish saying from that day it would be no sin for a human-being to kill and eat them. So we the *Rong*-folk believe from that day we can catch and eat fish, which we did not do when a fish was the wife of *Tashey-thing*.

So he was once more a widower, and he blessed us the *Rong*-folk, and said we should be as abundant as the bushes and trees in the jungle, and that until the monkey died out there, we should not die out.

And after blessing us, *Tashey-thing* returned once more to the country of the *Rum* (Heaven).

IX. The two Suns.

(*Told by Sonan-richen at Kasseon, April* 17*th.*)

1. *The toad kills one of the two suns.*

Once upon a time, there were two suns who were brothers. One rose at daybreak, the other took his turn at night, thus darkness was never created. The world, however, suffered a great deal from the tremendous heat, as it was always light; human beings and creatures could get no sleep. So they all took council together, deciding that one of the two suns should be killed.

The edible toad (the *tuk-blota-luk*), volunteered to kill the sun. He made an arrow from the red cockscomb plant (the *ka-num*), shooting the eldest brother with it. He died at once, his youngest brother becoming very sad, covering himself with a black cloth (the *chya-look-dum*).

It so happened then that the whole world was dark, one sun being dead and the other covered.

It became so black that the wooden pestles (*ta-ling*) turned themselves into snakes, the wooden mortars becoming Tigers (*tak-*

cham), and darkness is the cause of most of the evil in this world.[1]

The fire-flies (*tak-pit*) tried to lighten the darkness, but their light was not sufficient. A tree (*num-bun*) turned its leaves over, which were of a white colour underneath, but their light was not sufficient either. Half the human beings were killed by the snakes and tigers, so they and all the creatures implored the sun to take his cloth off, but it was of no avail.

And at last, even the *Rum* entreated the sun to uncover himself, but he would not listen to them either.

2. *The bat makes the hidden sun smile.*

Then the bat thought he would persuade the sun to uncover himself. He armed himself with a bow and arrow, hanging on to one end of the bow by his feet, while he placed the other end in his nose, saying to the sun in a nasal tone :—" If you remain covered much longer, through the intense cold the entire world will perish."

The sun became most anxious to see the speaker, for he reflected that out of the many who had come to see him, there had not been one who had spoken through the nose.

He looked down, and saw the bat hanging on to his bow upside down, so that he couldn't help smiling. As he did so, it became so hot that the bat lost his balance falling down to the earth. He fell on some stones, breaking many bones. That is why his feet are so different to any other bird or animal and why his nose is turned up.

3. *The toad punished for killing the sun.*

From that day, the sun shone. All the creatures took council in order to decide what should be done to the toad. They arranged that they would cut off his thumbs, and put him in a cold place. Unless this had been done, the sun would not have been pacified, and would never have given warmth to the world. In memory of the dead sun, names were given to the months.[2]

---

[1] Some tribes in Brazil believe that the night was sent to this world in a nutshell, and spread over the world causing darkness and misfortune when the shell was opened by mistake. Wicker baskets are then said to have turned into jaguars.

[2] The Lap-cha months are calculated by moons, of which they allot the usual twelve to the year. The month or moon is called '*laval*,' but the name of a month or period is '*nyom.*' The Lap-cha year is called a '*nam*,' and the new year starts in March. The new year '*nam-bu*' varies according to the date of the new moon, and according as the period is altered by the addition of an intercalary month, '*la-vo nyet*' or '*la-vo sho*' which is added about once in three years to regulate the lunar with the solar time. The names of the months are : (1) *ayit nyom* (March);

The dead sun became the moon, and in every seventh, eighth, or ninth month, the real sun sets very early, as he says he is tired. But the real reason is that during those months, the red cockscomb plant grows to its full height, and that he is afraid of being shot !

X. The Tiger hunted by Wind and Lightning.

(*Told by Chyung-gay at Lang-dang, May 5th.*)

1. *The wind and the lightning search for a wife, but are always refused.*

Once upon a time, there were two brothers whose names were *Yong-rumbo* and *Yok-gnibu*, who were both hunters (*sharabu*). Their sister's name was *Naremnom*. She was married to a tiger (*sa-thang*) who was called *Tung-bo*, and he had a brother called *Ren-lok-bu*.[1]

Now the tiger-brothers killed many human beings. *Tung-bo* used to fry their nails, and always gave them to *Naremnom* to eat which she enjoyed, but everybody began to hear of this.

Yong-rumbo and *Yok-gnibu* were travelling right round the world searching for a wife, but no one wished to give them their daughter, knowing *Naremnom*, their sister, was a man-eater, and thinking that one day, these two brothers might eat their wives.

They continually said they were not man-eaters, but people always told them to return and visit their sister.

So one day they found her, and saw that she was eating something. This they snatched away, and discovered them to be human nails. Thus they knew she was a man-eater, and became very angry.

2. *They decide to kill the tiger-husband of their sister.*

They said :—" You are a human but you are eating man's flesh, where is your husband, for we would like to see him ? "

The sister told them he had gone out hunting, but one of them turned into lightning while the other became the wind and they rushed about looking for him. At last they found him in the high mountains. They asked a bamboo (*payong*) who was near by to sit on *Tung-bo's* trail, but he at once asked them what his reward would be, were he to act as they asked. The two brothers told him that as his reward he would be allowed to take part in the ceremony of their sacrifice to the *Rum*.

---

(2) *ra-nyom* (April) ; (3) *mar nyom* (May) ; (4) *kur-nyit nyom* (June) ; (5) *kur-song* (July) ; (6) *thon nyom* (August) ; (7) *sam nyom* (September) ; (8) *num-tsam nyom* (October) ; (9) *blung nyom* (November) ; (10) *num-kum nyom* (December) ; (11) *pur-vim nyom* (January) ; (12) *glu nyom* (February).

[1] A snake which is found in the rocks.

So the bamboo sat on the tiger's trail, while the two brothers began to drive him. *Tung-bo* could not escape but followed the track which the bamboo guarded.

3. *Tung-bo killed, skinned, and his flesh scattered.*

When the tiger saw the bamboo bush in his way he asked him why he was sitting in his path, and asked him to move on one side quickly else he would be crushed. The bamboo did not move, so the tiger jumped on him, the stem of the bamboo piercing and killing him.

Then *Yong-rumbo* and *Yok-gnibu* came and skinned him, scattering his flesh in all directions, and the skin they carried with them towards the sunrise and the sunset in order to dry it.

And *Naremnom*, the tiger's wife, became very sorrowful when she heard of the death of her husband, and turning into a bird flew into the jungle weeping, to look for him.

And we Rong-folk believe she still lives, and can hear her weeping '*hoo-hoo*' in the jungle; and when we hear her at night we know that some calamity is going to fall on us.

XI. The Tiger and the Toad.

(*Told by Kam Sharap at Kasseon, April 17th.*)

1. *A tiger and a toad lick each other.*

Once upon a time, a tiger made friends with a toad, and as they always liked being together they went up one summer to the hills. When they came there, they rested near the bank of a lake, and the tiger hunted for lice on the back of the toad. However he could not find any, and at last the toad said :—

" Let me see if I can find any lice on you."

And the toad, finding many, commenced to lick the tiger's hairs in spite of them. At last he stopped and the tiger said :—

" Now let us vomit and see what we have eaten the last few days."

He vomited, but only small pieces of green leaves and white mud came up. When the toad vomited however, lots of tigers' hairs appeared. As the tiger saw this he was alarmed and thought : 'Now I am a flesh-eater, but I haven't brought up a single hair, the toad must be a tiger-eater.'

2. *The tiger, alarmed at the toad, runs away.*

So being frightened he ran away to the plains, and only stopped when he met a jackal, who asked him where he was going so hurriedly. The tiger told him he was running away from a toad, who had turned out to be a tiger-eater. The jackal could not believe this and said :—

" Do show me the toad, I would like see what he is like."

But the tiger was too nervous to think of returning, till the jackal said:—" Fasten this rope round your waist, and tie the other end round my neck, then we shall always be together, and you won't be frightened."

When the tiger had done this, he, with the jackal, returned to the hills, and they found the toad sitting on a stone, watching for them, as he thought the tiger would come back to see him. He nodded his head when he saw the jackal too saying:—

" It is three years since I sent you to find me some tigers, and now after all this time you return with only one! Come nearer and talk it over with me."

On hearing this the tiger became still more frightened, and ran down towards the plains dragging the jackal after him. When he arrived he found the jackal was dead as he had dragged him down by the neck the whole way. And that is the reason why tigers and jackals are never found in the hills to-day, but are always in the plains.

3. *The toad and the crow.*

At that time the toad became an enemy to the crow, who had once darted down on him, and had tried to kill him. One morning he caught him, but the toad said:—

" You ought to take me to the top of a hill, you know, if you want to kill me."

Accordingly the crow did as he was told, but when he set him down, and was ready to kill him, once more the toad said:—

" I am so very very thirsty, do find me some water before you kill me."

So the crow obligingly carried him to a pond, and after he had given the toad some water, he was going to eat him, when the toad cried:—

" As you are a priest (*yuk-mun*) you must say grace and thank God before you eat." And as that was true, the crow cried " Caw, caw," in prayer, leaving the toad. And whilst he was praying, the toad leapt into the pond and saved himself, and that is why we always find toads in ponds to-day.

And so we learn that a toad may frighten a tiger, but that he himself has to run away from a crow.

XII. The Tiger and the Ass.

(*Told by Aden at Gangtok, May 28th.*)

Once upon a time, the tiger, who used to come up to the Himalayas and kill and eat every animal he could find, met an ass.

The tiger asked him whether it would be possible for him to write—like he did on water—on the top of the *Kong-chhen* mountain.

The ass said however, he could on water only, and not on l and.

They came to a river, and the ass commencing to breathe and snort on the water, made most intricate and wonderful ripples, which the tiger tried his best to copy, but could not.

Then he asked the ass to come on still further with him, and wanted to know if he would cover the place for him where the herd of wild cows (*kyong-bik*) would break through the jungle, as he was going to hunt them. The tiger started to drive a herd he found, but it so happened it ran away quickly, and one of the wild cows fell over a precipice, rolling down to the spot where the ass was waiting at the foot.

The ass placed his foot on the dead body, which the tiger noticing thought he had killed.

"If he is able to kill such a big animal," he said to himself, "he could easily slay me!" And so he ran away again towards the plains, and from that time, he always stays away from the hill-country, and it can be noticed that though he often kills a pony or a mule, he never touches an ass.

XIII. The Tiger and the Jackal.

(Told by Chhylo-tabo of Santok at Sindhik, May 14th.)

1. *A jackal finds a dead elephant and invites a tiger to share the food.*

Once upon a time a jackal, who was wandering about came to a place where he found an elephant lying dead. He tried to eat the flesh, but could not tear the skin, so he passed in through the entrails and began eating. He couldn't find his way out however, though he had gone in easily, and hearing the sound of someone walking fast in the jungle, he cried out:—"If that is you, Brother *Sathong* (a tiger) come over here where the elephant is lying, and I will give you some of his flesh to eat." Brother *Sathong* came over, and tearing open the elephant's flesh he made an opening through which the jackal managed to crawl out.

Later he often went to the tiger's house, asking for the turn which was his due, though he was always careful to go when the tiger was himself out so that he need only bother the wife.

Now the tiger used to come home daily with meat which the jackal always took away, and the tiger's children having nothing to eat, grew thinner and thinner.

2. *The tiger plots to kill the jackal.*

At last Brother *Sathong* asked his wife if they had not sufficient meat. She replied they hadn't nearly enough as the jackal came everyday when he was away in the Plains, and took what he said was owed him. Then the tiger said:—

"If that be so, you must call him in to feed but I will hide."

That day the jackal came as usual, and Brother *Sathong's* wife asked him in to eat something.

"I will come in," the jackal said, "but I must sit with my tail hanging down between the bamboo stems."[1] The jackal managed to find a crack over which he could sit with his tail hanging down, and Brother *Sathong* rushed on him from his hiding place, but the jackal was too quick for him, and making a gap through the bamboo stems, he jumped down and ran away, the tiger following.

3. *The jackal causes the tiger's death.*

When the tiger was quite close to the jackal he ran up inside the hollow trunk of a tree. The tiger followed, but being too big for the hollow of the tree he stuck there, and after a few days he died. Meanwhile the jackal stayed up in the tree thinking the tiger was waiting down below for him, but when he became cold after death, and therefore much thinner, he fell down from the inside. Then the jackal came down, saw what had happened, and performing over the corpse of the dead tiger, he went back and told everything to his widow. She, however, would not believe him, so they went to find the dead body together. When they came to the spot the tiger's wife saw her husband lying dead, and said that as he—the jackal—had killed him, he would have to fetch meat for them all.

4. *The jackal tries to become a hunter.*

The jackal said he would do his best, and becoming the father of that house, he went out hunting everyday. But he could never catch anything, so collecting ants (*tuk-gnyom*) he gathered these up and brought them back.

The food, however, was not sufficient for the household, so the tiger's widow used to go out with the jackal hunting.

When they came to a big cowshed where there were many cows, she asked the jackal to kill them a calf. But he could not catch one, and ran about wildly from one to the other.

The tiger's widow asked him what he was doing, and he replied that he was looking for the fattest calf.

At last she herself was obliged to kill a cow, and she asked the jackal to help her to carry some of it, but he could not

---

[1] A '*basti*' is always built several feet above the ground supported by stone pillars. The floor is made of bamboo stems that are thrown loosely across horizontally.

even carry the cow's lungs without trailing them behind him on the ground.

When they came to a stream, the jackal could not cross and ran up and down the banks, till at last the tiger's widow cried :—" What are you trying to do ?"

" Can't you understand," he said, " that I am looking to see which is the shallowest part ? "

The tiger's widow, not knowing he dare not cross, went on with her children, believing him to be looking for the shallowest part of the river. When he jumped in later, the current caught hold of him, and he was carried away with it.

XIV. A Jackal tries to steal a Hen.

(Told by Shang-lui of Santok at Sindhik, May 15th.)

Once upon a time, there was a jackal living near an orphan boy. Now the orphan boy kept a hen, which the jackal wanted to steal. So early in the morning he came to him, and asked him where he was going to spend the day.

The orphan boy told him he was going to a field in the valley (a *dang-gnyot*), but instead of going there he went up into the mountains taking his hen with him.

The jackal ran down to the valley hoping he would be able to steal the hen, but he could not find it, and the next day he again came to the orphan boy, and asked him where he was going.

This time the orphan boy told him he was going up into the mountains, but he went with the hen instead to the valley. But one day he forgot to take the hen with him, and the jackal came and stole her, and when the orphan boy came home, he could find the hen nowhere.[1]

Meanwhile the jackal started to prepare his meal, and the orphan boy thought he would go and search for his hen in the jackal's house. On the way there he met a ripe *do-lom*, which is the fruit of the egg-plant, who asked him where he was going. He told him the jackal had stolen his hen and that he was going to find her, and the *do-lom* said he would accompany him, so they went on together. Then they met a needle who also asked them where they were going, and who followed them. They also met some cow-dung who ended by accompanying them.

When these four had arrived at the jackal's house, they found him dozing before the fire. The *do-lom* jumped into this, the cow-dung sat on the door-step, whilst the needle stood upright at the bottom of the steps.

---

[1] Cf. somewhat similar motive in Russian folk-lore. In this tale a cat appears instead of the orphan boy, a cock takes the place of the hen, and instead of the jackal, its northern equivalent the fox is given. See Gubernatis, op. cit., vol. ii, p. 59.

The *do-lom* burst suddenly, making the jackal jump. He started up, and after slipping on the cow-dung in the door-step, he fell on to the needle which pierced him to death.

So the orphan boy, and the hen escaped safely, and lived happily together for ever after.

XV. The Monkey and the Stork.

(*Told by Kam Sharap at Kasseon, April 17th.*)

Once upon a time, a monkey met a stork (*ka-dong-fo*). These two made great friends, they both climbed to the top of a tall tree, while the monkey said :—"Let us see who can shout the loudest," and hoping to frighten the stork he cried out loudly :—"*Kutsch-er-ik, kutsch-er-ik*" !

But the stork was not frightened at all, and only told the monkey to hold on to a branch when he screamed "*Kok-ko.*" He shouted, but the monkey not being at all alarmed, made him try again, so he called very loudly : "*Ko-ko-hang, ko-ko-hang,*" and the monkey in great fright let the branch go and fell down into the mud right up to his shoulders and found that he could not rise. Seeing a leopard who was passing at that moment he cried out :—" O ! leopard come and pull me out of the mud, for I cannot rise, if you put me on a stone I shall dry, and then you can eat me."

The leopard stopped, took the monkey out of the mud, washed him and was going to eat him, when the monkey cried :— "Don't eat me yet, do heat the stone first, I shall taste so much better if you fry me."

Whilst the leopard was heating the stone, the monkey cried :—"*Pari-na-gu-gu, pari-na-gu-gu,*" which is the Lap-cha monkey language for calling the wind.

The leopard asked him whom he was calling, and the monkey answered that he was shouting to him to make haste and warm the stone. Near by stood a bamboo tree, whose top was bending and which came nearer the monkey with every puff of wind. The third time he called, the bamboo branch was blown quite close towards him, and he caught hold of the stem and climbed up to the highest part of the tree. So he managed to escape, and cursed the leopard. And these two are enemies to this day, and we can see how furious a leopard always is whenever he sees a monkey.

XVI. The Bat evades paying Taxes.

(*Told by Chyope at Dickhu, April 25th.*)

Once upon a time there was a bat (*bryan*) from whom the birds demanded a revenue. When *Nun-bong-pono-ong-fo* (the king of the birds) demanded his tax, he showed his teeth, and snarled saying he was not a bird, but that he belonged to the family of rats (*ka-lok*) and would not pay any tax.

So *Komayi-pono* (the king of the rats) came to the bat with the queen saying :—" As you belong to the rat-tribe, you must pay taxes to me." But the bat replied that he was not a rat and did not belong to his tribe. " Look," he said, " I have wings so I belong to the birds."

Then *Nun-bong-pono-ong-fo* (the king of the birds) and *Komayi-pono* (the king of the rats) held a council and wondered if they should kill the bat as he would pay tribute to neither.

Hearing he was to be killed, the bat came out very early the next morning, and hung down on the corner of the thatched roof (*tum-kyan*) saying :—" The king of the birds and the king of the rats are going to kill me, they will shed my blood, so that means after my death you people will have a day of rest (*chyam-nyot*).[1] They mean to kill me, but I have a great many relations. My youngest brother is still at school, *Kan-thok-sang-po*, but there are seven others who are in the service of *our* king who will come and avenge me, I am sure."

Then he flew into the house again. When the king of the birds and the King of the rats heard these words, they became very angry, and fought together, but they made friends soon after, and spoke to each other on the following day saying :—" The bat must die, for he is a scoundrel."

The bat came out again then and repeated what he had said the night before, flying into the house once more.

Then the two kings flew and ran away deciding to leave the bat in peace, as he seemed to have so many friends who would all come and avenge him.

So that is why the bat is free from all taxation. Everybody in the world pays some sort of revenue, even we human-beings, but the bat is free and doesn't. That is why he always hides in the day time, and flies at night.

This is what we Rong-folk believe about the bat.

XVII. The Cat and the Rats.

(*Told by Chyope of Dikhu, April 25th.*)

1. *Some rats injure a Lama's clothes.*

Once upon a time there was a lama who was living in seclusion. At that time when the lama was in the dark, a rat came (*ka-lok*) and gnawed through all his clothes at home, and ate everything he could find in his larder (*chi-chhom*).

When the lama came out of seclusion he caught hold of the

---

[1] A day of mourning, *chyam*, vb., to shut, to close. *Nyet*, n., field, lit. to stop work in the fields.

rat, and asked him why he had so harmed him. But the rat denied having torn his clothes and eaten his food.

So that night, the lama set a trap, and found he had caught the rat when he went to look at the trap next morning. So to punish him, the lama cut off his whiskers and his tail, and then threw him into the gutter. And the rat said :—

"Although our king has many harsh laws, no one is ever condemned to lose his whiskers, and though there may be a severe religious law, no one's tail should ever be cut off. But you, a lama, have done both these things to me that are against the rules of either law, and so my people, and I declare war on you, and will come and do you much harm."

The lama replied :

"Very well, but if you do so, I will pray to the people in Heaven (the *Rum-lyang*) to defend me."

2. *The Lama prays for Divine Help, and a cat arrives.*

. Then he prayed to the *Rum*, and they dropped him a cat (*a-lyu*) down from Heaven that was wrapped up in a covering of dough (*a-pok*). As for the rat, he collected so many friends that in that part of the world there seemed to be nothing but rats.

Now a family of rats lived near the lama's house (*lee*) and they gave advice to this rat whose tail had been cut off and said :—"Listen, though you may harm lots of people you must never gnaw a lama's robe, or eat the things you find in his larder, for you will have much trouble, see if you dont !" But the rat answered them saying :—

"O nonsense ! a hundred of your words are not equal to one of mine, go and sit in the sun, and hunt for each other's lice !"

Then the army of rats came to the lama's house where they found him sitting in his usual place, and the head-rat said rudely :—

"You are in my way, get out, I wish to go to the other side of the room to see some more of my people, move !"

The lama moved quietly away, but the cat was starting to work.

3. *The rats get killed, one by one, all except the last one.*

The cat was, like the lama had been, in seclusion, and made the rats work for him, and bring him food. They went to him each in turn, one brought water, another carried firewood and they all waited on him. But they never returned, as the cat caught each in turn which he ate. Many of the rats thought it odd that none of the workers ever came back. They noticed the cat was becoming fatter. In fact it all looked very suspicious.

So it happened that all the rats were eaten except one. But one he could not catch, and it is from him all the rats are descended. If the cat had eaten him too, he would have gone up into Heaven but then, we should have had no rats.

And should a cat ever be killed, we, the Rong-folk believe it to be a very great sin as he came from Heaven. And it can be seen that though he is a flesh-eater, he tries to say his prayers when purring in his leisure hours.

XVIII. The Flea and the Louse.

(*Told by Abli Chyupan at the Ling-them Monastery, May 9th.*)

1. *The flea and the louse go to fetch firewood.*

Once upon a time, there lived a flea and a louse who were husband and wife. They purchased some butter, but couldn't light a fire when they returned home as they had no firewood. The flea said they would both go and fetch some, and whoever came back first should have the butter. They made themselves ready to fetch it, but the louse was so long shutting the door, that the flea was the first to get out.

When she reached the place in the jungle where she could pick wood, the flea had already found some, and was returning. But he has fastened the bundle to his back, and with every jump he took the rope broke and the bundle fell off, so that he lost a lot of time in re-binding it.

The louse came back quietly, long before the flea, and as they had arranged, she ate the butter, then after her long walk she felt tired, and went to lie down.

2. *The flea hits his wife, and calls a priest to cure her.*

When the flea returned and found the butter eaten, and saw that the louse was lying down, he became so enraged that he struck her on the body with a burning stick that he pulled from the fire. He did this only in anger, but the louse became so ill that he had to go and fetch a priest. The first traveller he met was a toad (*ta-luk*), who asked him where he was going. He said :—" My wife is very ill, so I am fetching a priest."

The toad said that he could do the work of a priest, and when the flea asked him to read so that he should hear the sound of his voice, he cried :—" *To-ak, to-ak.*"

But the flea did not like the sound of his voice, and walked away.

He next met a pheasant (*ta-ryok-fo*) who also asked him where he was going. The flea replied as before " My wife is very ill, and I am fetching a doctor."

The pheasant said that he could perform the duties of a priest, and when asked to pronounce some words, cried :—" *Ko-ko-chir, ko-ko-chir*, I read like this."

But the flea did not like the sound of his voice and walked on still further.

He next met a turtle-dove, who asked him where he was going, and to whom he replied as before.

When the turtle-dove said he could do the work of a priest and was asked to show a rendering of his service, he cooed :—"*Koo-yoo-koo, koo-yoo-koo.*" The flea was delighted saying :—"Your voice is the best I have heard," and took the turtle-dove home putting him in the most comfortable corner. He gave him '*chi*' to drink, and food to eat, placing the sick louse in front for him to look at.

3. *The turtle-dove devours the louse.*

The turtle-dove felt the day was very hot, and started pecking at the food, and drinking the '*chi*' which the flea had placed before him. At last he roused himself from his doze and asked for the patient.

The flea at once became rather worried as he remembered having placed the louse in front of the turtle-dove many hours before. He looked everywhere for his wife, but she was nowhere to be found. So, becoming very frightened and crying :—"*a-zi, a-zi,*" he hopped away jumping on to the human head of a man who happened to be passing.

From the top of the head he jumped to the nose, but thinking that the bridge of the nose was too high a mountain, he jumped into the mouth. Here he was frightened of the teeth that seemed to him a lot of huge stones, so he jumped to the belly where he thought the navel would be a good place to rest in. However many things fell on him here, and he thought that he would stay on the body no longer, so seeing a dog, he jumped on to its body, liking it much better.

So he stayed there, and that is the reason why fleas are always found on a dog's body to-day.

XIX. A Crab and a Water-wag-tail hunt a Stag.

(*Told by Chyanghe of Santok at Sindhik, May 14th.*)

1. *A crab and a water-wag-tail kill a stag, but a giant comes and snatches the body.*

Once upon a time, there was a crab and a water-wag-tail who made great friends (*ta-hi* and *sa-hem-fo*). One day as they were hunting, they met a pair of pheasants (*ka-hryak-fo*). The water-wag-tail thought they might hunt these two birds, but the crab said :—"No, let us wait until we find bigger animals." So they went on, meeting a deer with a fawn.

The water-wag-tail again asked the crab if they should not hunt these two, but he replied he wanted to find still bigger animals. So they went on again and met a large stag (*sa-ci*). The crab then covered the gap in the hedge which the stag would break through, while the water-wag-tail went into the wood to nunt him out.

As soon as the stag tried to escape through the gap, the crab caught hold of his neck and killed him. Then he took the skin off and offered it to the *Rum*. But a giant came to the spot, and snatching way the stag's flesh, he ate as much as he could, making the crab and the water-wag-tail carry the remainder to his house.

2. *These two kill the giant's wife.*

When they showed the meat to the giant's wife, she seemed very greedy, and the two friends said :—

"Shut your eyes and open your mouth wide."

But instead of giving her the stag's meat, they put stones into her mouth, crushing them down with a wooden pestle.

Soon after she died, and when the giant himself returned and asked them where the meat was, they told him that his wife had eaten it all up, and that she now lay dead.

The giant became so angry that he kicked the dead body, and the two friends ran away, but the giant followed them.

The toad came across a pond in which he at once hid, but the giant caught the water-wag-tail. He however prayed for his life, saying he would work for the giant, who let him go free, hoping to find the crab.

3. *The giant catches the crab who pretends to be dead.*

He was hiding in the water so the giant was not able to catch him, and he started to drink up all the water from the pond, first corking himself.

When he had nearly drunk the pond dry, the water-wag-tail darted down from the sky, and pulled the cork out, so that the pond once more filled up, and the giant was unable to find the crab.

Once more the giant started to drink, this time putting on a piece of sticking plaster.

The pond was nearly dry, but the water-wag-tail flew down again from the sky to remove the plaster. He stuck there however so the giant managed to catch the crab. He pretended to be dead, and the giant going home at once put him over the fire-place[1] where he was going to cook him.

The water-wag-tail found some cheese which had gone bad (*sal-dem*), and to pretend that the crab was high, he smeared him with it asking the giant to come and smell him.

---

[1] *Thop*—one of the three trays over a Lap-cha hearth.

The giant bent down to smell the crab, who grabbing him by the neck, pinched it till he died.

So the crab and the water-wag-tail took the place of the giant and his wife and lived happily ever after.[1]

XX. The Services of the Black Squirrel.

(*Told by Kanchyon of Har at Sindhik, May 18th.*)

1. *The orphan boy spares the life of the squirrel, and accepts its servitude.*

Once upon a time, in the *Lyang-bar* country, there lived two orphans, a brother and a sister. They lived in a shed which they had made from the tall green artemisia plant (*tuk-nyil*), and they had nothing to eat but the birds the boy caught by setting snares in a tree. Lots of these birds were caught by a black squirrel, and then on those days they would have nothing to eat.

One afternoon they were very hungry, and the boy saw the squirrel take a bird that was caught in one of his own snares on the tree. He drew out his knife (*ban*), and followed as closely as he could. Without letting him out of his sight he ran up and down three mountains until he came to the banks of a big river. There he caught the squirrel up, who was so tired he could not move. The squirrel implored the boy to spare his life; if he did not kill him, he would work for him all his life. The boy spared the squirrel's life who became his slave from that day.

2. *The squirrel procures a Chinese princess as a bride for the orphan boy.*

One day the black squirrel asked his master to travel towards the sunrise (the *tsuk-car*).

On their way to the country in the East, they passed the river where the Chinese Princesses (*Gyanogk*) bathed. Just then she had left her clothes on the bank. When the black squirrel was some way off, he noticed this, and he asked his master to wait a few moments.

He wanted to take all the princess's clothes away, but she implored him not to. The black squirrel wouldn't at first listen, but at last said to her if she would only listen to what he had to say, and give her consent to it, he would give her the clothes he had found, otherwise he would run away with them. She promised she would and then he said :—" With me there is a young man, will you run away with him ? If not—."

[1] It is singular to notice that in Greek folk-lore, the crab, the stag, and the nightingale are usually associated together, they are mentioned in magic cures, etc. (cf. Gubernatis, *op. cit.*, vol. ii, pp. 338–359).

The princess wanting her clothes back, consented immediately, but the black squirrel said :—" Promising is good, but not sufficient, swearing is better, put one of your hands in the river and swear you will accompany us, and will not return to your palace." She put both her hands in the river, and the oath was so great the river dried up. But the black squirrel was not satisfied, and he told the princess to swear with her hand on a tree. This she did, and the oath was so great that the tree withered. Still the black squirrel was not content, and he told her to swear putting her hand on a rock. So the princess put her hand on a big rock that was standing near by, and swore, and the oath was so great that the gigantic rock split in two. Then the black squirrel returned the clothes to the princess, who put them on and returned with him to the orphan boy. He went on ahead carrying her box full of ornaments and saying :—" Master and mistress, follow my footprints."

3. *The squirrel comes to a cow-shed, and declares it to be the property of his master.*

The black squirrel went on uphill until he came to a cow-shed where he put the box on the ground, and rested asking for some water crying :—" O-hoo-o-i," and asked for some water.

The cow-boy invited him to have some refreshment and to drink '*chi*,' but he answered that he was in a hurry, or he wouldn't be panting in the manner he was. So the cow-boy only gave him water to drink, and the black squirrel said :— " The King of *Lyang-bar* is coming, so don't be unprepared, you must put everything in readiness for him."

On hearing this, the cow-boy made the shed tidy, and made sitting-places for the two when they should come. When the orphan boy and the princess arrived and sat down, the black squirrel said to them :— " This is my master's cow-shed."

They stayed there for one night, and on the following morning, they prepared for their journey again, the black squirrel asking them to follow his footprints.

4. *They come to the palace of the seven demons, whom the squirrel slays.*

The black squirrel went on up the hill until he came to a large building looking like a palace (*dee*). In it seven demon brothers lived (*Dut*), who were called the *Anchkentobo*. In front of the palace he once more put down his box crying :— " O-hoo-o-i," and asking for some water. The seven demon brothers asked him in to have some refreshment, but he replied he was in too great a hurry to eat, and just wanted some water. They gave him some and then he said :—" You seven demon brothers have given so much trouble to all the human beings, and to all the animals, that the *Lyang-bar* king is coming to kill you with all his army. I come to tell you of this as I am your friend."

On hearing this the demon brothers became restless, and started looking for hiding places, but the black-squirrel said :—" You won't be able to hide yourselves anywhere because his soldiers are like an army of ants and will hunt you out anywhere. Only follow my advice and perhaps I shall be able to help you."

He asked some of them to dig a big hole, some to make a three stone hearth, some to fetch water, and the remainder to collect fire-wood.

When they had all done their work, the black squirrel advised them to hide in the big hole they had made as the army was soon coming. They all jumped in, and as they were crouching down hiding, and the fire-wood they had collected had made the water boil, the squirrel threw it over them, killing them all.

After doing this he went inside the palace, and removed all the dead bodies of the human beings he found in the larder which showed that the demons were cannibals. Then he made all the other rooms comfortable in the palace, and soon after his master and mistress arrived.

First of all the black squirrel led the princess to the larder telling her it was all his master's meat she saw. Next he showed her the wardrobe and he told her all the clothes she saw were his master's. Then he showed her the gold and silver rooms, and all the cooking vessels, and told her that everything belonged to his master.

When she saw all this the princess was very astonished as she had no idea the black squirrel's master possessed so much property and wealth. She was pleased and excited, and they lived in the palace whilst the black squirrel cooked for them.

5. *The orphan boy's sister is brought by the squirrel.*

One day he told the princess he was going to fetch his master's sister who lived all alone a long way off, and had only a few cows to look after in the *Lyang-bar* country. Taking some of the clothes from the wardrobe, and some food, he arrived at the shed, and found his master's sister dying of hunger. But he managed to bring her back to the palace where he introduced her to the princess, and told them they should live happily together.

6. *The squirrel returns to the Rum.*

So twelve years passed and the black squirrel had been his master's slave the whole time.

"I have served you all this time" he said, "but I am from the *Rum* country, and must now return, give me permission to leave."

But his master wouldn't let him go, and he stayed for another three years. And though he repeatedly kept asking for leave, they kept him for another four years, when he said he would have to leave. But even then they tried to prevent him escaping, so he sent them to sleep knowing they would dream and prayed saying:—"Should the clouds separate when I ascend to the *Rum* country, we shall know that we are all to meet once more on this earth. But if they remain closed, we shall know we are only to meet in Heaven (*Rum-lyang*)."

The black squirrel was then wafted up to the blue skies, and as he was taking off all his earthly elements entering into Heaven, the three he had left awoke.

They were searching everywhere for the black squirrel in vain, when they cast their eyes heavenwards and saw him being swept upwards. They watched him until he was covered by dense clouds, and then they knew from their dream they would not meet in this world again, and they wept. But after their time of mourning they lived happily ever after.[1]

XXI. A Fairy disguised as a Puppy.

(*Told by Yanku-sarang Mandal at Kasseon, April 18th.*)

1. *An orphan boy spares the life of a big fish.*

Once upon a time there was an orphan boy who had nothing to eat but the fish he caught. One day he happened to catch a very big fish, and as he was dividing it up in his mind's eye into equal portions for several days, it spoke. "Don't kill me," it entreated him, "come with me to my father and mother instead." The orphan boy said:—"But how can I go with you into the water?"

The fish told him he would have to hold on to his tail very tightly, and jumped with him into the river swimming until they came to his father and mother who were sitting on golden and silver thrones. The fish explained he had been caught, but the orphan boy had been merciful. The father and mother fish told the orphan boy they were happy and grateful, and would give him as a recompense anything he desired.

2. *He receives a puppy*[2] *as a reward, and brings her home.*

The orphan boy noticed a wee puppy lying in a corner of the hearth, and asked them to give him this. He brought it back to his cottage, and tied it up in a corner.

[1] A variant to "le chat botté," see Gubernatis, vol. ii, pp. 60-61.

[2] The parallel motive of a fairy assuming the form of an animal, such

As usual he went out every day, but when he came back every evening he found everything was ready for him. His food was always cooked and waiting for him, though he never knew who worked. One day he hid himself in a corner to see who would come in. He saw a beautiful girl, who appeared when the dog took off its skin. She was made of gold from her head downwards, and from her waist downwards she was made of silver. She started to cook but the orphan boy came out from his hiding place, took hold of the puppy's skin and tearing it into pieces, scattered it everywhere. Gold and silver flowers sprang up where it fell.

But the girl said :—" Alas! my time has not yet come," but the orphan boy would not listen to her entreaties and from that day they lived together in that cottage.

3. *The King sees the puppy-wife and wants to have her.*

One day the King of that country saw the beautiful girl, and taking a great fancy to her, he desired her for his own. " Alas! " cried the girl once more to the boy, " if you had only listened to me and waited—now much trouble will fall on us."

The King said to the orphan boy :—" Let us have a cock-fight, and whoever wins shall gain your wife."

When the orphan boy heard this he wept, and said to the girl :—" I am but a poor man and haven't a bird fit to fight the King's cock." But she said :—" Do not worry but go to my father and mother's place in the river, and ask them to give you the medium-sized cock."

So the orphan boy went to the girl's parents in the river, and returned with the medium-sized cock. The next morning at sunrise the cocks were let loose on the playing ground, and when they fought it so happened the King's cock was killed.

" This time," he said, " you have won, now to-morrow we will have a bull-fight."

When the orphan boy returned home, he wept again, saying to his wife " But where can I get a bull ?" But she told him to go to her parents and ask for the medium-sized bull. He went down to the stream, swam and came back with the bull. The next

---

as a frog, puppy etc. is very common in folk-lore. Cf. Gubernatis, *op. cit.*, vol. ii, pp. 26, 377–383.

The motive of a contest between the King and one of his subjects with animals is a favourite subject in the *Lap-cha* tales. In another story heard at Kasseon by *Sharap lama*, (April 19th) the King tries by similar means to take the wife of one of his subjects. This time she is not a fairy, but she was " so beautiful, that if she were placed in the sun she would melt, or if she were placed in the shade, she would freeze." But the contest this time is of a different kind. They arrange to try the effect of food on their digestion, and also attempt to resist the unusual secretion of saliva at the sight of the opponent eating sour fruit. The 'orphan boy' inevitably wins, apparently without any supernatural help, and 'lives happily ever after.'

morning at sunrise the bulls started fighting, and the King's bull was slain.

The King became very angry at both his cock and his bull being killed, and said that for the third time they would fight themselves with armies.

This time the orphan boy wept louder than ever, as he was all by himself, and had no army, but the beautiful girl told him to go once more to her parents, asking for the medium-sized box. He received it, and on the next morning as he saw the King coming towards him at sunrise with a big army, he opened the box. Lightning flashed out of it, killing the King with all his men.

Then the orphan boy became King in his place, and lived happily with the beautiful girl ever after.

XXII. The Food-producing Skin.

(*Told by Gyaten Tachung at Phensang, May 25th.*)

1. *An orphan boy is given the magic skin as charity.*

Once upon a time there was an orphan boy who wandered from village to village, and from town to town. Once he found that the inhabitants of one of the villages had killed a sheep, and he asked for and obtained the skin which he kept in his shed. Every day he went out to work. When he returned home, he found everything was always prepared for him: his meals were cooked, while drink was also provided.

Just then it happened that his rice crops which were ready for harvesting had been destroyed by monkeys and rats. He hunted these and managed to catch a monkey and a rat, which he was going to kill, only they both cried out:—"Have mercy on us and spare our lives for one day, we shall be useful to you." So the boy spared their lives, and went away to the river. There he raised the traps he had put in the stream to catch some fish, but in the place of any fish he only found a big toad. This he was going to kill when it cried:—"Have mercy on me, and spare my life, for one day I shall be useful to you."

2. *A demon attempts to steal the skin.*

Near by there lived a demon who had 18 heads, and when he heard there was an orphan boy in the village who had a skin which could produce any food required, he swore he would get it from the boy, so one day he went to the cottage and stole away the skin.

When the boy returned to his shed, and discovered his loss, he called the monkey, rat and toad, and said he now required their help to try and get his skin from the demon who had stolen it. The monkey, taking the rat and toad on his shoulders, went to find the skin, and they found the demon who was near it, asleep.

The skin was hanging up on a rope, but the rat ran up the rope which he bit with his teeth just above the skin, so that this fell to the ground. Then the monkey started carrying them all on his shoulders,—the rat, the toad and the skin.

3. *The skin is dropped into the river, but recovered.*

They came to a big river, but the monkey thought if they were careful not to talk, he would be able to swim across. He put the skin in his mouth, and telling them to be sure and be quiet he commenced swimming.

Midway, both the rat and the toad began to ask the monkey questions. These he took no notice of, but at last the rat bit his ear, and he had to open his mouth and speak so the skin fell down to the bottom of the river. It went down, they think till it reached the other world.

The toad said :—" I think I shall be able to help you, but you must go on until you meet a woman with her spinning rod. Once you get this, I shall be able to start working."

The monkey went on till he met a woman spinning, and she readily gave up her spinning rod when the monkey asked her for it. The toad asked his friends to wind the thread round his body, and to hold on to the other end of it the whole time.

They led the toad down to the very bottom, and he found the skin which he brought to the bank of the stream. Then they arrived at the orphan boy's shed, the monkey carrying them as before.

They gave the skin to him, and as they put it down on the floor a lovely girl stepped out.

She told the orphan boy to shake the skin inside and outside the shed. Wherever he did this, gold and silver coins sprang up out of the ground. Many guards and servants appeared, so that the orphan boy found himself very rich, and he and the lovely girl lived happily ever after.

So we learn the *Rum* (who are the gods who cause happiness) won, while the *Mung* (who are the evil demons who cause sorrow) were defeated.[1]

XXIII. The Last Goat's Tail.

(*Told by Sata Penlok at the Phensang Monastery, May 25th.*)

1. *A woman saves the tail of the last goat in the herd.*

Once upon a time there was an old man and an old woman who had 100 goats, which the old man used daily to herd.

---

[1] The Lap-cha words that always end a story.

Once the old woman asked her husband how many goats they had, and he answered they had about five times twenty. In some days more she again asked him how many there were, and he answered "Four times twenty." Later she again asked him and he replied :—"Now we have three times twenty." When she asked for the fourth time, he said there were only twice twenty, and when she asked him for the fifth time he said :— "Now we have only twenty." The next day the old woman went to see the goats, but to her grievance there was only one. Asking her husband the reason, he told her they had been eaten up by a leopard. The old man thought the best thing to do would be to kill the remaining goat, but his wife disagreed, and protected it holding on to the tail which she held in both her hands until the old man had severed it from the body.

This she placed in a box and returned home leaving the old man who stayed behind to eat the goat.

2. *The tail is saved from being cooked by promising its labour.*

When he came home too, he asked her whether she had eaten the tail. It replied itself however from the box saying where it was. The old man went to the box, and taking the tail out tried to place it on the fire. It however spoke again, and asked him to have mercy on it, and said that later it might be of use to him.[1]

The next day the tail asked for a bamboo water-vessel (*pa-dam*), and although it was small it filled up all the other vessels. Then he asked for a bamboo basket (*tung-jang*), and brought it the next day full of fire-wood (*schang*). Though it was small and carried little, it completely filled up the shelf where the fire-wood was kept. The next day he said :—"Now I am going to kill some bullocks, the King of *Lyang-bar* has left for you in the jungle."

3. *The tail goes to kill bullocks.*

When the tail went out, he found the sun so hot that he sat down in the shade of a mushroom. Two Princes happened to pass by, one was of the sunrise and called *Tsuk-lat*, while the other was of the sunset and was named *Tsuk-that*. They thought they would use the mushroom as a target, and they

---

[1] The *Garos* treat the tail of a goat as the most essential part of the sacrifice. It is placed on the top of a plate of rice, and is soaked in the blood of the victim. (*Gazetteer of Assam*, X, p. 32.) The idea has apparently the same meaning as that of the last sheaf in the field. This is always regarded as the refuge of the spirit of the corn. In this case it is probably the spirit of the herd. Cf. J. Frazer: *The Golden Bough*, vol. vii, p. 268, and vol. viii, pp. 10, 43.

nearly hit the tail who cried out :—" O! you two nearly had me, I am just resting here." Then the two Princes went to see who was calling, and they found the tail who asked them where they were going.

The Princes replied they were going to hunt the three bullocks in the jungle belonging to the *Lyang-bar-pono*. The tail told them he was also going on the same errand, and suggested they should all go on together, and as they came near the cattle-shed the tail went on alone. Hiding beneath the tails of the bullocks he cried out making the cowherd come out three times before he went to sleep to see if anyone was about. Then the two Princes came up, and killed all the bullocks which they carried between them, as the tail was only able to carry some of the blood in a bladder. The tail then told the two Princes if he shouted they would have to run away, and as they would be pursued it would be better were they to leave their load behind them.

4. *The tail steals the three bullocks killed by the two Princes through a trick.*

When they drew near the tail's home, he shouted as loud as he could, so that the two Princes ran away leaving their loads behind. Then the tail went in to the old man and woman, telling them he had brought a present, but it was so big he had had to leave it outside, and that they had better go at once to fetch it in. He asked them to boil the meat on the stove, and to fasten the heads on the roof, meanwhile he would go to fetch the *Lyang-bar-pono*.

Then the tail called at the Palace, and the King asked him why he had come. And the tail said :—" I wish to pay my respects, and ask you to come to a meal in our humble home." Then the King went back with the tail and had a fine feast. As he was eating, he looked up and saw the three bullocks' heads on the roof. Then he realized they had been stolen from him, and that he had eaten his own meat.

The tail noticing his upward glance said :—" You keep things you never want, and I am only showing you how you may benefit others."

5. *The tail undergoes an ordeal, and is ordered to steal guarded treasure.*

The King said :—" If you are able to remove my treasure (*serdong-pa-tek*) from its box this evening, I will do nothing, and should you remove it, you may marry my daughter, the Princess, but should you find you are unable to do this, you will have to replace my three bullocks."

That evening the King ordered his Palace to be well guarded, and placing four guards at each corner, he said no one should enter after sunset. At night the tail came, and noticed the guards were all sleeping, so he let the hounds loose, replacing them by sheep, and he placed sticks in the guards' hands instead of their bows and arrows. He entered, to find some more men sleeping in the kitchen, and stole into the bed-chamber of the King. He found he had not slept all night, but was holding the treasure in his hands. Once when he went into another room, he handed it over to the Queen, saying she would have to be very careful with it as that night the tail would probably come and steal it.

As soon as the King had left the room, the tail entered and said that after all the Queen had better hand him over the treasure as he thought it would be safer with him. The Queen thinking it was the King, handed the treasure over; and when the *Lyang-bar-pono* returned and asked for it, she said :—"But you took it just now as you left the room." So the King guessing the tail must have the treasure shouted to the guards, who found they had no arms, and when they wanted to let the hounds loose, they found they had only sheep.

The tail managed therefore to get away with the treasure, which he showed the next day to the King, who was obliged to give him the Princess as he had promised.

6. *The tail arranges three dances and appears in human form.*

One day the tail asked the Princess and the old woman to go to a dance the *Lyang-bar-pono* was holding on the top of the hill near by. He told them, going up, they were to take the short cut, but on returning they were to use the zig-zag track. As they left, the tail followed, and though he took the longer zig-zag path he arrived first. It was he who was holding the dance though the Princess and the old woman didn't know, and as he returned quickly by the short cut whilst they took the long zig-zag track, they found him at home when they returned.

The Princess and the old woman went thus three times to the dance, but on the third time the Princess suspected the tail and hid herself in the cottage.

She saw the tail become a King, and leave the cottage with many followers.[1] So picking up the tail which she found lying on the floor, the Princess threw it on to the fire. The smell of its burning reached the King, who returned home hurriedly. He told the Princess his time had not yet come, and that she had done wrong in burning the tail so soon, but she had better shake the remains of it quickly in every corner of the cottage. Wherever the Princess shook the tail, the whole place was filled with

[1] Cf. a somewhat similar motive of a goat-husband's metamorphosis. Gubernatis, vol. i, pp. 410-411.

gold and silver, numbers of men, horses, and herds of cattle sprang up out of the ground, and the place became equal to the Palace of the *Lyang-bar-pono.*

C. *Heroic Legends.*

XXIV. The *Golden Knife* and the *Silver Knife.*

(1) A King's unsuccessful hunting. (2) The King dozes and misses the stags. (3) The King marries the youngest daughter of the *Lung-da* ruler. (4) The King brings his bride home. (5) The King starts on a journey, and during his absence the twins are born. (6) The plot of the witches to destroy the twins. (7) They do much mischief in the palace. (8) The return of the King. (9) Execution of the twin's mother. (10) The hungry dog. (11) The grandfather unearths the twins. (12) The miraculous building of the palace by the twins. (13) The King summons the twins, sending messengers to fetch them. (14) The twins are sent to fetch the golden and silver flutes from the demon. (15) The twins go to the demon's home, promising to return in nine years. (16) The golden boy climbs up and steals the flutes. (17) He hits the tusk with a stone from the sling. (18) He is pursued by the demon. (19) The *Golden Knife* falls dead but is resuscitated. (20) The demon is also resuscitated. (21) Exchange of magical instruments. (22) The heroes return home. (23) The twins reveal the mystery of their birth, and punish their witch-sisters. (24) *Ramit-pandi* resuscitated and the witches executed. (25) The two boys wrestle, are killed and resuscitated.

XXV. *Ga-bu* and his horse.

(1) *Ga-bu* makes friends with the wife of the demon. (2) *Ga-bu* plots the destruction of the demon. (3) *Ga-bu* is poisoned by the demon's wife. (4) *Ga-bu* and his horse fly up to the *Rum* country.

XXVI. The adventures of *Ati-azyak.*

(1) The King asks the diviner to pray for a son. (2) The deities decide which of their sons has to be re-incarnated as the King's son. (3) The birth of *Ati-azyak.* (4) *Ati-azyak* with his six brothers go to marry the seven daughters of the king of *Lung-da.* (5) *Ati-azyak* visits the sea-serpent. (6) *Ati-azyak* comes before the serpent-king. (7) *Ati-azyak* starts on his errand with the help of the serpent's wife. (8) *Ati-azyak* comes to the land of the seven demons with whom he has a contest. (9) *Ati-azyak* plays Hide and Seek with the seven demons. (10) *Ati-azyak* contests with the demons—using fighting animals. (11) *Ati-azyak* with the two queens starts on his return journey. (12) *Ati-azyak* punishes his brothers and kills the demon. (13) *Ati-azyak* returns to the *Rum* country.

XXVII. The adventures of the merchant-widow's son.

(1) The merchant-widow's son receives a luminous flower. (2) The flower is presented to the king. (3) A beggar comes with promises to befriend the boy. (4) The boy starts on his errand. (5) He comes to the land of the Paroquets. (6) He comes to the land of the Peacocks. (7) He comes to the *Sambi-ula* palace, that is inhabited by five demons. (8) The boy steals some flowers and leaves with the maiden.

(9) The five evil demons are drowned. (10) The boy returns home, bringing the flowers. (11) The king orders the boy to build a palace. (12) The boy is ordered to explain the origin of the *Tista* river. (13) The seven try also to visit the *Rum* country but are killed.

XXVIII. How *Ling-Gyaso* subdued all the devils.

(1) He is re-incarnated in the world. (2) *Ling-gyaso's* miraculous birth. (3) The baby is given to the demons whom he kills. (4) *Ling-gyaso-gya-bo* goes to the devil's country. (5) The king returns home and kills his uncle. (6) *Ling-gyaso* goes to the country of *Hore* and kills the uncle. (7) *Ling-gyaso* kills *Hore's* son. (8) The king's return and his fight with *Hore's* minister.

XXIV. The Golden Knife and the Silver Knife.

(Told by Chyodi of Ringen at Mangen, May 3rd.)

1. *A King's unsuccessful hunting.*

Once upon a time there lived a King who was called the *Lyang-bar-ung-bar-pono.*[1] He had no queen so he spent his time hunting, and always had his two dogs with him, *Kshibu Tum-chung* and *Tum-chhen.*

He killed much game and his larders were well stocked. One day it so happened he saw nothing, there was not even a bird flying in the jungle, and at sunset he returned home in the dusk, thinking of the many animals he used to kill and how to-day he had killed nothing, and becoming very morose he went to sleep. The next morning at cockcrow he woke, and thinking of his bad luck the day before he went on to the palace balcony to see the view at sunrise. In front there lay a meadow named the *Pemo-pettong* and on it he saw two stags grazing, a mother-stag with her foal, feeding in turn one side of the meadow, and then on the other. Thinking they were probably the cause of his ill-luck of the day before, the King went inside meaning to prepare for hunting, and cooked some food giving his dogs a share, who however would eat nothing.

The King told them they had better eat as they would be hunting but they replied :—" No, don't go out hunting to-day."

The King would not listen to them however and said :—

" Unless you follow me as usual to-day and hunt, I will cut both you in pieces when I return."

And the dogs thought : " As we shall be killed to-day, whether we hunt or not, we had better follow our master."

---

[1] *Lyang-bar,* meaning the middle part of the country, *ung-bar*—the middle part of the sea.

2. *The King dozes and misses the stags, whom he follows to the Lung-da country.*

They ran round the meadow thrice while the King watched the place where the animals would break cover. But becoming very sleepy he dozed, and he did not see his dog *Kshibu Tum-chung* chase the stag towards the *Pho-chu* and *Mo-chu* Rivers. While the other one followed the fawn towards the *Lung-da* country. The dogs met both the animals together at the turning of the path, and these turning into she-devils, killed the two dogs, leaving both bodies on the ground with their heads pointing towards the King's land.

Sleeping, the King dreamt the dogs had returned and were fawning on his arm, then suddenly waking up he roused himself, and realizing the animals had broken cover, he followed their footmarks. Coming to the spot where the four animals had met, he saw the dead-bodies of his dogs, noticing the footprints of the she-devils which were as large as plates. He became very angry, and said with feeling :—" Whoever it is who has killed my two dogs, him will I follow and kill in revenge."

3. *The King marries the youngest daughter of the Lung-da ruler.*

When the King came to the palace of the King of *Lung-da*, he greeted him and then noticed that there were two fairies there who were sisters named *Se-lamen* and *Tung-lamen*. It was the eldest who attended to him that night, *Se-lamen*, and he laughed to himself thinking how he thought he had been following two devils, and how he had discovered two fairies! He thought he would make great friends with *Se-lamen*, and sleeping with her that night, he asked her what magic deed she could perform.

The fairy told him she knew of one grain of rice with which she could feed the King, and all the people in the Palace including even the dogs. After hearing this, the king longed for the morning, and he spent the whole of the next day wandering round the Palace. The second night he spent with the youngest fairy *Tung-lamen*, and asked her to tell him what magic she could perform. She said she only knew that from one roll of cloth she could clothe the King down to the lowest person in the Palace, even making coats for the dogs and mats for the hens to lay their eggs on.

The *Pono* (King) also heard the King had another daughter, the *Ramit-pandi* (Queen), whom he had shut in a room ever since her birth.[1] The King thought he would also

[1] See elaborate information concerning parallel motives of the seclusion of girls in folk-lore, J. Frazer. *Golden Bough*, vol. x, pp. 70–76.

like to go and find out whether she knew of any magic deed, and that night when everybody was asleep in the Palace, he found her room and entered. When he asked the Princess at first what magic she knew of, she denied knowing any, but when the King urged her, she at last said :—"But were I to tell you, even the walls might have ears, also the time may come when you will change, and you will say you no longer love me."

But the King promised he would always love her, and implored her to tell him. Then the Princess said :—"I only know of one magic deed, I can give birth to a golden knife and to a silver knife."

The *Lyang-bar-pono* when he heard this was very happy and said he would marry her.[1] But when she told him the two fairies had been listening, and when they heard that she could give birth to a golden and to a silver knife, they laughed and clapped their hands, saying that if she could do such a thing, they would be able to also, and they ran away.

4. *The King brings his bride home.*

The next day the *Lyang-bar-pono* asked the *Lung-da* King for his daughter, as he had no wife or children, and the King said if he truly loved the *Ramit-pandi* he had no objection. The *Lyang-bar-pono* said he truly loved her, so the King promised him her hand.

Several days passed and the *Lyang-bar-pono* brought many valuable gold and silver gifts from his own country to give the King of *Lung-da*. He had asked the Princess to accompany the King back to his home, had given her a great dowry, and was sending many men and horses to accompany her. These were looking forward to travelling with the Princess, but the two fairies said :—"You need not go with the Princess because we shall escort her."

The King's followers were sorry when they heard this, but they were obliged to stay behind. Thus the four came to the country of *Lyang-bar*, and for a while the *Ramit-pandi* lived very happily. The time came when according to her promise she became fruitful, and the King thought he ought to prepare food and clothes for the child's arrival.

---

[1] In a Russian folk-tale this motive appears almost word for word: three sisters have nearly the same extravagant way of speaking (but the youngest promises to give birth to a hero—not to twins). The king incidentally overhears their conversation and marries the youngest sister. In the further development of the story, the same elements also appear, in the absence of the king the queen gives birth to a boy. She and the child are thrown into the sea by her sisters who accuse her of having given birth to a monster. Cf. also Gubernatis, vol. ii, pp. 30-31.

5. *The King starts on a journey, and during his absence the twins are born.*

He told the Queen he would be very busy, and started on his journey to buy the necessary things. Just as he was leaving he hung a bell (*shyong-sa-tibu*) above her pillow, telling her she was to ring it as soon as she had become a mother, when he would at once start to come to her. Were the bell to ring at night he would reach her in the early morning, and were he to hear it at sunrise, he would be with her in the evening, even if he were on the other side of the world, he would, wherever he was, start back at once.

Soon the Queen's time came when the pain started, it became so great she felt it in the tips of her fingers, and in the tips of her toes. Then she gave birth to the golden knife and soon after to the silver knife.

As soon as the golden knife fell to the ground, it cried three times, and the sound was heard by the eldest fairy, while as soon as the silver knife fell, it cried three times, and was also heard by the youngest fairy.

6. *The plot of the witches to destroy the twins.*

These two then plotted and said :—

"Our enemies are born, the best thing we can do is to put them out of the way at once."

So they went to the *Ramit-pandi's* room, pretending to help her in her illness, but as she slept they hid both the children in an earthen pot they brought with them, and closed it down with 19 layers of cotton-wool. Then they tied the neck firmly, fastening it with rope that had been made from a yak's tail, (*salong-thak-po*), and sealed the knot with the *Lyang-bar-pono's* seal. Then the two fairies carried the earthen pot to four cross roads each facing north, south, east and west. Here they buried it beneath the 12th layer of the earth which they covered over with ashes, and satisfied themselves by placing a flat heavy stone on the top, returning home and feeling happier now both their enemies would die.

7. *They do much mischief in the palace.*

They entered the *Ramit-pandi's* room saying :—

"Now you are an invalid, we will look after you, and we will first of all brush your hair."

So they made her sit up in bed, and combed her hair with iron combs. They combed so hard that the *Ramit-pandi* was scratched from head to foot so deeply that you could see her heart and lungs. As she was lying on the bed half-dead, they brought in a bitch-puppy which they put to her breast, hoping it would look as if the puppy had scratched her. When they had done this they found the food which the *Lyang-bar-pono* had prepared and ate it. They also killed all the *Ramit-pandi's* bullocks and cows, eating the flesh and throwing the bones in a pile until they reached half way up the Palace. They broke open the door of the *Lyang-bar-pono's* rice store, cooking and eating all the contents till the water they strained from it became as big as a sea. Then they opened the *Pono's* '*chi*' store-room, and both witches drank till the millet seeds they threw away grew into a heap as high as the Palace itself. After that they broke open the store-room, where the tea was kept, and drank so much that the heap of used tea-leaves mounted higher than the Palace.

8. *The Return of the King.*

After eating all this they walked into the *Ramit-pandi's* room, and rang her bell that she had been told to ring. The *Lyang-bar-pono* King heard it when he was busy buying clothes for his expected child in the market of the Black Plain (China, *Gya-nock*). As he heard the sound he ran towards the Palace with great joy, wondering whether it was a girl or a boy. When he arrived the two witches laughed and clapped their hands saying :—

"See the result of not marrying one of us, go and see your golden knife and your silver knife that are now feeding on the *Ramit-pandi's* breast. We are from the *Rum* country, but instead of marrying one of us, you chose her. She must have been living with a dog as she has given birth to a puppy."

The *Lyang-bar* King at first would not believe the story and went up to the *Ramit-pandi's* room. There he saw the puppy feeding at her breast, and saw scratches all over her body. The witches told the King to look at all the refuse heaps, the pile of bones, the sea of rice, the heap of millet seeds, and told him the *Ramit-pandi* had devoured it all and said she was not one of them, but was a devil (*sa-mo*), and they advised the King to tie a rope round her neck and to drag her as far as the *Pho-chu* and *Mo-chu* Rivers, where he should cut her head off. When the King saw all this he believed the fairies, and becoming very angry, he tied a rope round the *Ramit-pandi's* neck, dragging her along to the two rivers, and followed by the two witches who threw ashes after her.[1]

9. *Execution of the twin's mother.*

When they came to the bank of the *Pho-chu* and *Mo-chu* Rivers, the two witches asked the *Pono* to find a wooden

---

[1] Ashes are thrown after any one who is suspected of being an evil spirit; the same is done when any one's name is mentioned who has been cursed. Ashes thrown after any one are said to cause their death. Cf. Hastings' *Encyclopaedia*, vol. i, p. 426, where a similar custom amongst the *Araucanians* is referred to. The idea of throwing ashes is to make the ghost miss his way.

block on which he could place the *Ramit-pandi*'s neck to cut her head off. This he did putting the head and body into the stream. But as soon as he had done this, and the current was sweeping the body downstream, the head floated upstream towards the rivers' source and the two witches cried :—

" This is an evil omen, the *Ramit-pandi* must have left something undone in this world, she is not at rest, and they both started throwing stones at the head which commenced praying saying :—

" I would I could see my two orphan children again, if only they could get out of the earthen pot, we could meet in human form once more."

Then the head floated downstream.

The two witches became queens to the *Lyang-bar* King and lived in the Palace.

10. *The hungry dog.*

And in those days at the Palace, the servants and the dogs could not get enough to eat, so the servants ran away and the dogs died. There was only one old bitch who remained, she thought : " When our former mistress was alive she gave me so much food that I had to leave some as I could not eat it all, now I am starving so I had better go."

Before leaving she howled three times, and set out not knowing which way she was wandering She came to the ridge of a mountain where she rested a short time, and looked round. In the valley far below she saw a lean-to and thought if she could only reach it she would be able to get some food. So she dragged herself along and managed to crawl to the shed, but when she reached there she found that the door was shut. However going round, she managed to make an opening through the leafy wall. Once inside, she looked for some food but only found an empty plate. Looking up she saw a shelf on which a cracked earthen pot was standing containing a little millet flour. Being very hungry she jumped at the shelf hoping to reach the flour, but the rope holding it gave, and she fell with the pot on the floor, all the flour being scattered. The earthen pot was broken, and she found little to eat, but wishing to see the owners of the shed, she went to sleep in the corner.

When the sun was setting, the bitch saw an old man and an old woman coming up to the shed from the valley. They seemed to be both very tired, and when they had entered the hut the old man lay down on one side of the hearth, whilst the old woman took the other side. After he had rested some time the old man said :—" Well Grandmother, why don't you get up and cook us something ?" As he spoke he pulled out a jungle vegetable (the *kan-tong-bi-gnyom*) from his pouch (*kasok*) handing it to her, whilst she pulled out another one (the *kamchel-bi-gnyo*) from the folds of her dress (*dum-pin*).

The old woman thinking that she would boil these two vegetables, turned round to fetch the earthen pot from the shelf, when she saw that it lay scattered in pieces on the floor.

She woke up the old man, saying that a thief had entered the hut and that they must look for him. The Grandfather rose, walking round outside, but saw only the footmarks of a dog. It seemed to have come inside, so entering again, he looked round and saw the black bitch in a corner. As soon as he saw her, he cried out:—"It is you who are the thief, it is you who have broken the pot and scattered the flour, why should I not beat you, why should I not kill you?" He lifted his walking stick (*kar-patung*) high above his head, when the dog said entreatingly:—"Have mercy on me and don't beat me, go and ask my master to replace the broken pot and scattered flour, for I must belong to somebody."

Then the old man asked her who her master was, and hearing it was the *Lyang-bar* king, she was not beaten but the old man went to see the king as the dog had suggested.

11. *The Grandfather unearths the twins.*

When he arrived outside the Palace he shouted:—"The king's dog has broken some poor people's earthen pot, and scattered their flour, so I come to demand their replacement."

The two witches heard him shouting and came on to the balcony, where they saw the old man, and made him repeat what he had said. They told him the best thing he could do would be to go to a certain cross road, which they pointed out to him, and to dig in the centre where he would find an earthen pot containing enough food to last him his life. They also advised him to carry the earthen pot straight to his hut, and not to bring it to the Palace.

The Grandfather became very glad, and went to the meeting of the four cross roads, hoping he would find his recompense. When he came near the spot he heard children laughing, and clapping their hands, but when he reached the centre he saw nothing and could not find the earthen pot. Thinking the two Queens must have lied to him, he turned back towards the Palace again, and had taken three or four steps when he heard the children's voices once more, and turning round quickly he heard them laughing and clapping their hands again.

He came near the centre of the cross roads, and could see nothing but a stone lying there, this he removed with the aid of his stick finding an earthen pot in a hollow underneath.

This he took out, and breaking the seals round the neck, and cutting the rope, he found two boys inside who were as beautiful as the sun and moon.

The Grandfather became very pleased, and placing the earthen pot on his head like a cap, he put one child in his *kasok* while he held the other in front of him with his hands, feasting on him with his eyes. Every few paces he took, he would change them about, placing the one he had been carrying in his *kasok*, and holding the other in his hands.

When the old man came to his hut, and the old Grandmother saw the children, she became very happy too, while the dog bowed down to them in respect, and from that day the two old people's hut was always full of food, and they had no trouble, so that in a very few days they became quite rich.

One day, the Grandmother asked the Grandfather to give her one of the boys. At first he would not; however, she implored him to, and at last he gave her the youngest *Komhankub*, telling her to look after him very carefully. So from that day the youngest slept with the Grandmother, while the eldest slept with the Grandfather.

12. *The Miraculous Building of the Palace by the Twins.*

One day they said to the two old people :—"Now during this night you will hear a great deal of noise, you must keep very quiet, and not open your eyes, and must not ask the cause of the disturbance."

At midnight the two old people heard a great deal of noise. It came from the side where the sun rises, from the side where the sun sets, from the *Rum*-country above, and from the country of *A-nok* (Hell) below. They heard the sound of men cutting stones, dragging posts and building while in the morning the old Grandfather was lying in a golden bed, whilst the old Grandmother was in a silver one. The boys who were sleeping with the two old people roused them, and when they saw they were in golden and silver beds, they could not believe it was not a dream, and putting their tongues out in astonishment found they could not put them in again. The two boys said :—"Don't be frightened, this is the Palace you two are going to live in."

With great wonder the two old people climbed out of their beds, and in their haste to get on to the balcony, they ran into the cupboards and against the walls. When they stood on the balcony, they found the Palace stood on exactly the same place as the hut had done.

"You need not wonder at all these things," the boys said, "the *Rum* built it all for us in a single night."

Then the old Grandfather, and the old Grandmother lived happily in the Palace which was finer than the *Lyang-bar* king's.

13. *The King summons the Twins, sending messengers to fetch them.*

The twins went out to play in a flower garden in front of the *Lyang-bar* king's Palace. Among all the other flowers there was a bush called the *chambar,* where many birds called the *sang-dyam-fo* were sitting. The twins aimed at these, killing many which they stuffed in a bag.

As they were shooting, the *Lyang-bar* king came out on his balcony and saw them. He was astonished at their beauty as they might have been the sons of a King. He watched where they would go, and wondered at never having seen them before. The next day the twins took the cattle out grazing, and led them to one of the *Lyang-bar* king's fields.

The King went out himself to see what damage they had done, and saw the Palace on the same place where the hut had once stood, and it seemed finer than his own. He sent a messenger to call the old people to him, but before the messenger had arrived, the eldest boy knew that he was coming, and told the old people not to be frightened at the messenger's arrival as he would answer all the questions. In the meantime he made the front of their Palace as muddy as if a lot of cattle had just trodden there. The *Lyang-bar* king's messenger came, and standing on the top of a stone to be free of the mud he cried to the old man and woman :—" You two had no cattle a few days ago, now you have a great many, you had no Palace before, and now you have this one, but the cattle have done much damage to our fields, and the king of *Lyang-bar* summons you to appear before him."

Now the messenger had a very good cloth on, and as the elder boy came out of the Palace, rays of light shone from him and his beauty, so that the messenger became blinded and fell off the stone into the mud.

The boy said to him :—" As you are the messenger of a King, you should be able to see your way about better," and put him into the sun to dry, after saying to him :—

"You had better return now, tell the King the old people will appear before him."

When the messenger returned to the King, having a muddy cloth, the king of *Lyang-bar* asked him what had happened. He answered :—" O King, the boy we were searching for yesterday is staying over there in the Palace, and when he came out he shone so brilliantly, I found I could not stand in his rays, and I fell down in the mud." The King said :—" If you saw the one boy, the other must be also staying there. I do not want to see the two old people now but the boys," and he sent another messenger to fetch them.

So another messenger came to see the two old people who was an officer of a higher rank and dressed therefore in a finer cloth. Coming to the stone which the other had stood on, he cried :—" The two boys are summoned now by the king instead of the Grandfather and Grandmother."

The elder brother came out again, and as soon as he had reached the door, rays flashed out from his beauty again, so that this messenger started and fell off his place of refuge into the mud, and the boy picking him up said :—" As you are also the King's messenger, you should be able to see your way about better," and as he put him into the sun to dry, he told him that the two boys would obey the king's order, and would come and see him at sunrise on the morrow.

When the King of *Lyang-bar* heard the boys would be there the next day, he made his Palace ready for them and prepared a great feast.

14. *The twins are sent to steal the golden and silver flutes from the demon.*

At sunrise when the boys appeared, people they met could not stand before the rays shining forth from them, so that everybody fell down, but the twins raised them up by their arms, asking them if they stooped down in order that they should not see.

When they reached the Palace, the King of *Lyang-bar* begged them to sit on the golden and silver thrones he had especially prepared for them, but they refused to do either, and looking stern, the elder boy sat at the foot of a golden pillar, whilst the younger boy sat at the foot of a silver one.

Then the king asked them about their father and mother, and from whence they had come, but the twins answered they had no father or mother and had come out of the earth in an earthen pot, so that they must be the sons of the earth. But the king repeatedly asked who their parents were, and said the earth and earthen pot could not be their father and mother.

The twins kept saying they did not know who their parents were, the only thing they could say for certain was that the elder brother knew their bone had come from the country of *Lyang-bar*, while the young one said he knew their flesh had come from the country of *Lung-da*.[1]

Now all this was heard by the two witches and they guessed the old man had dug up the earthen pot from the ground in the centre of the cross roads, giving the twins their liberty, thinking they had better kill, as soon as they possibly could, because they would be their enemies, they advised the King to kill the twins at once, otherwise they

[1] The *Rong*-folk believe it is the father who gives bone to his offspring, while the mother gives flesh and blood.

would grow up to conquer him, and would become the King, of *Lyang-bar*. They also said he could not kill them without reason, so he had better place them in the hands of the demon (*dut*) *Chenchhyo-byung-pono*, telling the twins to steal the demon's pair of gold and silver flutes. As a reward he told them that they would be made Kings of *Lyang-bar*. The King thought this was all true, and ordered the twins to fetch the pair of flutes from the demon.

The boys said to themselves :—"The King could not kill us himself, and he is only sending us to the demon to be killed, but we must obey his order and either fetch the flutes or die in the attempt."

15. *The Twins go to the demon's home, promising to return in nine years.*

So they set out for the demon's country, and the old people were very sad at their departure saying :—

"These twins are just like a drop of foam, so immature. How can they fetch the pair of flutes when so many Kings and heroes have gone there never to return. But the twins gave them hope saying :—

"It is not certain we shall be killed, only give up all hope if we do not return before nine years."

Then they left for the demon's country *Chenchhyo*, carrying a pair of yaks' tails with them, one being black and the other white. They went on and on until they came to the ridge of a hill, and from that distance they saw the Palace of the demon. When they reached it they saw the demon-king lying asleep, one of his ears making his pillow while the other covered him like a blanket. The two flutes were in his mouth, one on each side, and he was holding the ends of them in his hands.

The younger brother said at once he would get the flutes, but his brother told him he was too young, and when they had had their lunch which the Grandmother had put in a bag for them, the elder brother jumped up to fetch the flutes.

16. *The golden boy climbs up and steals the flutes.*

Before he left he told his brother that when he had the flutes he would run away towards the Black Plains of China (*Gyanak*) and towards the White Plains (India), but that the demon would follow him, and then he would *ascend to the sky*, and would drop down dead, falling on the upper side of the road, while the demon would fall down dead on the lower side of the road. The moment he fell down dead, he, the younger brother, would have to wave three times up and down his body, with the black yak's tail, passing it from his head to his feet, and then he was to wave the white yak's tail, passing it from his feet to his head.

The elder brother went up to the demon, and started to climb up him from the toes to the head. When he reached the knee, he was so tired he had to sit down and rest, and then with great difficulty he continued his journey as far as the breast. There feeling very tired and hungry, he had the remains of his lunch from the bag. Feeling refreshed he went on his way reaching the neck and climbing on towards the mouth, he found he had at last come to the flutes. First he took up the golden one, then he made his way to the silver one, returning the same way he had come. As he stepped off the demon's foot, and came to the ground he thought that though he had the two flutes he would like to get one of the demon's tusks.

17. *He hits the tusk with a stone from a sling.*

These were so long that they touched the sky, and he thought he had better try and break one. So putting a stone in a sling he aimed at the tallest tusk, which broke off falling to the ground.

This woke the demon up, and the boy, seizing the tusk and the two flutes, and putting them over his shoulder, turned and ran. The demon followed him crying :—"You have not only stolen my flutes, but you have also broken my tusk, when I catch you I will eat you!"

18. *He is pursued by the demon.*

But it so happened the demon could not run fast, his balance being upset through the loss of his tusk. Owing to the same reason, he failed to catch the boy when he snapped at him with his mouth. The boy ran towards the sunrise, and towards the sunset, towards the north (the *Lho*, the Highland), and towards the south (the *Dang*, the Lowland), with the demon following him closely. Then the boy *ascended to the sky*, and the demon flew up too making a noise like thunder.

19. *The Golden Knife falls dead but is resuscitated.*

The younger brother who had been watching the whole time thought his brother would be killed. Both of them seemed very tired, and then, as he had been told, his twin brother fell down on the upper side of the road, while a short time after the demon fell down on the lower side. Remembering his instructions, he went over to his brother's side taking the black yak's tail with him which he waved three times, passing it from the head to the feet. He also waved the white yak's tail three times, passing it from the feet to the head. Then the elder brother woke, and they were once more together. When they had had lunch the younger brother said :—" As we have the two flutes, let us return to our own country," but the other brother said :—" We ought not to leave the demon in this state, it would be better to wake him up too." But the younger brother said :—" If we do, he may devour us," but the other answered :—" It is better to wake him up as he may be useful to us later."

20. *The demon is also resuscitated.*

So he took up the yaks' tails, and waved three times with the black one, passing it from the feet to the head, and he waved three times with the white one, passing it from the head to the feet. This woke the demon up, and instead of devouring them, he bowed before them and said :—" You two must be very good men, in fact heroes, for you have had mercy on me, and have spared my life, if you will allow me to invite you to my Palace, I should like to make friends with you."

21. *Exchange of magical implements.*

So they went to the Palace, feasted and made merry, and made great friends. The demon asked them to tell him the magic of bringing the dead back to life, but the brothers said they did not call it magic, they only used two yaks' tails, and they explained the method which had to be used on human beings and demons. The demon full of astonishment and wonder said :—

" As it is so simple, will you exchange the two yaks' tails for my walkingstick, and my rope made from the hair of a yak ? " (*kar-patung* and *salong-thakpo*).

The two brothers asked their use, and the demon replied if they ordered the stick to beat anyone, that would it do, and whatever they ordered the rope to bind that would it fasten.

So the two boys were willing to exchange the two yaks' tails for the demon's stick and rope, and prepared to journey back to their own country. As they were leaving, the demon said that one tusk was of no use to him and cutting the other off himself he asked them to accept it. The two brothers took it and asked the demon to come to them at the moment of their death, and said they would come to him whenever he died, and taking the two flutes and the two tusks they returned to their own country.

22. *The heroes return home.*

When they reached it, they found their Grandfather and Grandmother mourning for them, and covered with dust and ashes. The two boys woke them and said they had returned, but at first they would not believe them and said :—"You two have just come to deceive us, our two boys have gone to the demon's country, and we do not think they will ever return." But the two boys answered :—"No, Grandfather and Grandmother, it is really your two boys, we have returned from the demon's country and are just the same." The old people looked at them out of the corner of their eyes, and when they saw they really were the same two boys they jumped up from their couches happily and hastened to bring food. That night they stayed very cosily all together, and the next morning the two boys said they would go to the King of *Lyang-bar* to give him the two tusks and the two flutes. They had provided the old people, they said, happily for their lives, and they had come to subdue the King's enemies. They then ordered the rope to hide beneath the threshold of the King's main door, and told the stick to hide himself below the hearth. They said they would tell the king of *Lyang-bar* about their parentage and birth, and when they told him this, the two witches would try to run away. As soon as they reached the threshold, the rope was to bind them, and then the stick was to beat them. The stick would beat so hard, their bones would come out, and their flesh would go in. So the stick and the rope started on early the next morning.

23. *The Twins Reveal the Mystery of their Birth, and punish their witch-sisters.*

Carrying the flutes and the tusks the two boys went towards the Palace of the King of *Lyang-bar* the next day, and when they reached there, they rested one of the tusks against one of the corners of the Palace, and it was so heavy that the wall fell down. The King of *Lyang-bar* and the two witches ran on to the balcony hearing the noise in alarm, and saw the two boys standing there. When the two witches saw they had returned from the demon with the flutes and the pair of tusks, they became frightened as they guessed the demon would kill them at once and they both ran inside again quickly.

The boys came inside the Palace and told the King they had brought him the demon's pair of flutes he had wished for, but they knew now he had simply sent them there to be killed.

The golden boy sat at the foot of the golden pillar and the silver boy sat at the foot of the silver pillar, both looking very stern, and refusing to have anything to eat. The King asked them again about their parentage and if they came from the side of the sunset or from the side of the sunrise, from the country of the north (*lho*), or from the country of the south (*dang*). But the twins replied that all they knew about their birth was that they had come from the earth in an earthen pot. However the King insisted on hearing the truth, and at last they said :—

" Do you remember the day you went out hunting, and lost your two dogs, how you found them lying dead, your visit to the king and your questions about magic to the two fairies, and do you not remember the *Ramit-pandi* told you she could give birth to a golden knife and to a silver knife ? "

The King said he could remember all these things, but it was a puppy *Ramit-pandi* had given birth to, so he had killed her and had put her body into the river.

Now as they were talking the two witch-sisters became frightened, and after talking it over they decided they had better fly away at once, and they made themselves wings out of their dress-folds (literally the loose end of a Lap-cha dress forming a sort of bag when held out, a *dum-pim*).

While they were hastening to make wings, the twins told the King although he had a big head, he had few brains and although he had a large breast he had no heart. The two fairy sisters were really she-devils, they themselves had been the *Ramit-pandi's* sons.

" At the time of our birth," they told him, " she had nothing to eat, those heaps of bones and millet seeds with the sea of rice water were the remains of what the two she-devils had devoured. They put all the blame on our mother, and buried us in an earthen pot at four cross roads, and we were saved by a dog who had taken shelter in the hut of two old people. But here too," they added, " you tried to kill us, as you put us into the hands of a demon. We have only just now been saved from him, and have returned."

Meanwhile the two she-devils had come out to fly away from the Palace, but the rope bound them on the threshold, while the stick began beating them so severely that their bones showed and came out, while their flesh sank in and it nearly killed them.

However the twins wanted a little life left in them, so the rope became slack and the stick stopped beating, and then they asked the king to fetch their mother.

But the king was very frightened, and ran about trembling hither and thither. He ran down towards the rivers, but did not see the *Ramit-pandi* anywhere. Three times he ran down and three times he came back, but each time he could see nothing.

24. *Ramit resuscitated and the witches executed.*

The twins asked the King to give them two sieves and two iron rods, and when he had brought these two things they told him to carry them down to the rivers where their mother had been killed. This he at once did, whereupon the twins went a little downstream, and began to stir the water till the stones at the bottom started to roll, while the sand and mud rose. They then drained the water through the sieves, the younger brother catching two hairs, one blue and one white, whilst the elder brother caught a piece of bone. After washing these they brought them to the Palace where they placed them over an incense burner, purifying them in the smoke. Then they placed them in a bamboo stem, with a bow and arrow (*sa-lu chom*) and a spinning rod (*lasyu*) closing it up and saying :—

"If it is possible for us to meet again, we would like to see you re-born in three or four days' time; if you are re-born a boy we will find you shooting with the bow and arrow, and if you are re-born a girl, we shall find you using the spinning rod."

They hung the bamboo stem on the golden post, and on the third day when the twins were listening for sounds in the bamboo they heard the whirl of the spinning rod. They prepared a seat, and then opening the bamboo stem they found a girl whom they discovered was eight years old. She came out and sat down in the seat they had prepared. The two boys were very happy, as they had found their mother again. They sat on her knees, one on each side, drinking milk from her breast, the elder brother was on the right side whilst the younger brother took the left.

On the next day, the *Ramit-pandi* asked them to bring the two she-devils before her, and then taking up the comb she scratched both their bodies and put puppies to suck at their breasts. As the puppies were sucking amid the heaps of bones, millet seeds, and tea leaves, she asked the King to tie ropes round their necks and to drag them towards the *Pho-chu* and *Mo-chu* Rivers, and as he was pulling them along she took up a handful of ashes which she threw after them saying :—"From this day you shall have nothing more to do with the country of *Lyang-bar*, and you are thus driven out of the land."

When they had all come to the bank where the two streams met, the King brought up the wooden block on which he had killed the *Ramit-pandi*. The twins cursing the she-devils, asked the King to cut their heads off. He did this and the twins cast their bodies into the water, and from that day the she-devils existed no longer.

The others all returned to the Palace, and the King, the *Ramit-pandi* and the twins lived happily ever after.

25. *The two boys wrestle, are killed and resuscitated.*

The two boys were always playing. One day as they were wrestling, they fell off the balcony on the upper storey, and fell down to the ground, both being picked up dead. The father and mother were mourning and feeling very sad.

Now the wind brought the message of the two princes' deaths to the demon *Chen-chhyo-brong-mung*, and as they had formerly promised to attend the death of each other, the demon hastened to the country of *Lyang-bar*. He thought that he might be able to help his two friends and carried the two yaks' tails with him.

He arrived at the Palace, and found the father and the mother weeping over their two sons' dead bodies. Taking up the yaks' tails one after the other, he started waving them about as he had been directed, and they both came to life, and rose up, the younger brother however turning into a girl. Then the demon was given a feast, and a bullock was killed. They boiled this whole without taking out the entrails, cooking as well eight big pot-fuls of rice, also giving him eight big bamboo vessels of '*chi*' (*pa-thyut*) which they had strained.

All this the demon ate in mouthfuls. Then when he had bidden them all farewell, the two children said :—"You have no enemies and you will reign peacefully in your country, *Chen-chhyo-brong*." So he returned, and both kingdoms had peace. The son took the name of the *Dyu-zong-bo-pono* (king), while the sister was known as the *Zelem-pandi* (queen).

No one was as happy as these two, and they had revenues coming to them from the lands that stretched from the sunrise to the sunset.

XXV. Ga-bu and his Horse.

(*Told by Sadam Tsgring, Kalimpong, Sept. 7th.*)

1. *Ga-bu makes friends with the wife of the demon.*

Ga-bu was riding his favourite horse, and as he was riding up a steep path, he met the demon called *A-tschung-mung-la*, whom he thought of teaching. They talked it over, and came to *A-tsdhung-mung-la's* Palace. There the demon went out shooting leaving *Ga-bu* alone with his wife in the Palace.

She was weaving two pieces of cloth in turn, one was of silk, while the other was woven from the jungle nettle plant (*ka-su*).

Now *Ga-bu* was dressed in the poorest of clothes, and looked like a beggar, but he asked her what she was going to do with the cloth when she had finished weaving them both.

The wife told him she would give the plain nettle-plant cloth to her husband, but she would keep the silk one for *Ga-bu* in case he ever came to see her.

2. *Ga-bu plots the destruction of the demon.*

Then *Ga-bu* told her who he was, and asked her to let him know in what places her husband's spirit lived. She would have to question him closely, and he would hide near by where he would hear everything that was said. He also asked her to feed his horse for him which he had tied to the top of a hill ; he had put several bunches of grass in front of it, but these might not last if he were away a long time. The horse he had named *Chongse-gu-bu.*

Hearing the demon *A-tschung-mung-la* returning, he looked round to see where he could hide, and crept in the hollow trunk of a tree opposite the Palace.

When the demon's wife questioned her husband about his spirit's place of abode, *A-tschung-mung-la* asked her why she wanted to know: it might mean she wanted to kill him. But she said:—"O! you go out hunting so often that I want to please your spirit that it may then bring you good luck."[1]

So the demon told his wife that his spirit lived in a pine tree in front of the house (*tung-sing-kung*). It also lived in several small fish she would find in the stream that ran near the house (*ta-hrim*) and that it also lived in the body of a honey-bee. So she must be very careful never to cut the pine tree, kill the fish or hurt the bee. Should she do so, he would of course die.[2]

Thus *Ga-bu* heard everything, and when *A-tschung-mung-la* went away again, he came out of the hollow trunk and wickedly cut the tree down, killed and cooked many of the fish and caught the bee which he burnt in the fire.

When the demon returned, he was groaning as if in great pain, and soon after he lay down and died. *Ga-bu* at once cut his head off, which he kept, giving the body to his widow.

3. *Ga-bu is poisoned by the demon's wife.*

Then *Ga-bu* lived in the Palace, but the demon's wife gave him poisoned '*chi*' to drink one day, and after taking that he slept for three years. The demon's wife then covered him with dried mud, and used him as a hearthstone with three hearth-stones on his chest to cook pots on. He woke up at length and the demon's wife then gave him poisoned food, and he slept for three more years. At last she wished him to go away, and when he again woke up she sent him to find his horse which was still tied up in the same place. The demon's wife had given him iron maize to eat, and had amused herself by beating him. It was so long since he had been tied up, trees had grown up all around him, and as *Ga-bu* came near him he started to run away. His master followed him, and noticed that the nearer he approached him the trees grew smaller and smaller. Whilst he was running

---

[1] This is practised by the Lap-cha, who calls it '*mung-suk,*' i e. exorcising an evil spirit.

[2] These details have been studied by J. Frazer—the destruction of the external soul with the treacherous behaviour of the wife, the story of the demon, or the giant, whose destruction is plotted, etc. See *Golden Bough*, vol. xi, pp. 95–152. In the Lap-cha tales it is a frequent motive (cf. No. xxi).

away he caught some bamboo leaves, and the elephant grass (*pa-sor*) which to this day have *Ga-bu's* horse's teeth marks on them.

4. *Ga-bu and his horse fly to the Rum country.*

And then *Ga-bu* managed to reach him just as he was leaving earth to go to the *Rum*-country, he even had his two front feet off the ground—but *Ga-bu* caught hold of him and asked him why he wished to go so soon to the *Rum*-country, if he went, he, *Ga-bu*, would like to go there with him.

Chongse-gu-bu then told him the demon's wife had been very cruel to him, and had been giving him iron maize to eat which had caused him very great pain. To believe this *Ga-bu* had only to slit his stomach open when he had gone up to Heaven.

And the horse wanted to leave this earth and to die, and he asked *Ga-bu* for his knife (*ban*), as if he wouldn't kill him he would stab himself. *Ga-bu* gave him the knife, and the horse stuck it in the ground with his teeth, then falling on it and killing himself.

To see whether the horse had been telling the truth, *Ga-bu* cut him open, and found a lot of the iron maize inside. So he knew that the animal had spoken truthfully and he felt very sad, and after burying him he decided he would go up to the *Rum*-country too. Thus they, *Ga-bu* and the horse both flew up.

XXVI. The Adventures of Ati-azyak.

(*Told by Chyupan at Sindhik, May 16th.*)

1. *The King asks the diviner to pray for a son.*

Once upon a time, there was a king of the *Lyang-bar* country [1] and his queen *Tung-kung-ramit*, which means she was as radiant as a rainbow (*tung-kung*). They had six sons and no daughters.

Now the king was very restless and uneasy, for whenever men came to settle in that land, they were found dead on the following morning. He wished to find out the reason, so he went to a diviner named *Aku-sangyo-yuk-mun* taking a wealth of gold and silver with him.

Aku-sangyo-yuk-mun told him he would have to go into meditation for seven days, and that before retiring he would have to bathe. Were he to do so, the diviner said, he would receive one more son, who would do much good. He must also sacrifice a great deal of *phuchi* and *muchi* (a sacrifice of birds and fish), and give drink (*chi*), rice (*zo*), cooked rice (*ta-fa*), and ginger (*heng*), which he would have to offer on a bamboo carpet (*samok-talu*).

---

[1] The country lying in the centre of the universe supposed by the Lap-chas to be Sikhim.

So the king went into seclusion and made the sacrifice as the diviner told him, and watched and waited for a saviour to be born.

2. *The deities decide which of their sons has to be incarnated as the king's son.*

In the country of the *Rum*, the sweet incense of the sacrifice was scented by the *Rum* father and mother, who both hastened to find the place it was ascending from. The *Rum*-mother found the room where the incense was rising as it was filled with perfume. She became very happy and told the *Rum*-father how very fragrant the incense was, but he said:—"Yes, it may have seemed sweet to you, but the king of *Lyang-bar* wants us to send him a son in exchange for it, so it means we shall have to part from one of our three sons." He called them and said that whoever was strong enough to lift the stone lying on the playing-ground (*lingmu-partem*) should be sent down into the world to be a son to the king of *Lyang-bar*.

The two eldest brothers became exceedingly joyful, and at sunrise the next morning they wished to throw the stone, but found they could not lift it.

Then the youngest brother thought he would try (he was still sucking his mother's breast) and he went to the playing-ground saying:—"May the stone rise as soon as I touch it if it is I who am to go to the country of *Lyang-bar*," and picking it up easily, he threw it as far down as the world (the *Ling-lyang*).

The two elder brothers seeing this became angry, and beating their younger brother and leaving him behind they came and told their father that they had thrown the stone. However, the *Rum*-father told them there was another test which they would have to perform. "Behind the twelfth mountain," he said, "there is a needle, go and aim at it and whoever hits it will be the *Lyang-bar* king's son."

At sunrise the next day the brothers went out, but the two elder ones could not discover where the needle lay. "May I strike the needle," the younger one said, "with my first shot if I am to go to the *Lyang-bar* country." He drew his arrow and struck the needle at once, which angered his two elder brothers. They beat him again, and left him behind, saying they had hit the needle, not their youngest brother.

Their father told them that for the next test they had to make tea. "You are to put it in a bamboo cup (*kha-tak*) and before the steam rises to the top of your head, you must try and split the hair of a horse's tail," he told them. The next day, they all tried this and the younger brother again won.

Then the father told them he would be the son of the *Lyang-bar* king who could collect enough food and firewood quickly which would be sufficient for the remainder of their lives.

The brothers all tried on the following day, the two elder brothers fetched only one load of firewood each, but the younger brother brought many bundles back.

Then the father asked them what they should all want if they went down to the *Lyang-bar* country. The two brothers at once said they would want much gold and silver with a herd of horses, a herd of cows, and a flock of sheep, but the younger brother said all he needed would be his father's sword (*pa-yuk*), his invisible hat (*gyu-shambu*) and his golden hat (*zer-yalu-shambu*) and a cow, a mare, a hen and a goat that were all blind in one eye So he was chosen, but at the last moment he couldn't help weeping going away from home, and his mother slapped him so hard that he fell down dead. At the same moment the cow, the mare, the hen and the goat died, and with the younger brother they all found themselves in *Sari-rung-dong-chen*, the country that lies midway between the *Rum* country and *Ling-lyang*, the country that is the world.

Here looking down below he saw the Queen *Tang-kung-ramit* weaving on a loom. Seeing this he dropped water on her so that she was forced to take shelter. Doing this three times he, with all the animals, became one large hailstone, and fell down by her side. The Queen seeing this cried out :—" O! you have been troubling me so much," and breaking a piece of the big hailstone, she swallowed it, throwing the rest away. These in turn were swallowed by a cow, a mare, a hen and a goat who all had young.

3. *The birth of Ati-azyak.*

But the queen *Tang-kung-ramit* gave birth to a bag one day which alarmed her and she buried it in some cross roads near by.

Just at that time the king of *Lyang-bar* was outside the Palace looking where the child would be born. He could not find it, and returning home he found his wife lying down though no child could be seen. He asked her to tell him the truth, and promised no harm should come to her if she told him everything. The queen at once told him about the burial place, and the king running quickly to the four cross roads could find nothing. Then he heard a voice crying :—" Father do take me out very soon." He heard the sound coming from the earth, so he dug down, finding the bag which he immediately cut open. Inside there was a copper pot which had a cover. In that he found a lovely boy, a son, and becoming very happy he returned home with him.

The next day he invited many people whom he feasted and asked to find a name for his son. No one could find a suitable one however, and the king at last chose a name suggesting *Ati-azyak-pono;* this pleased everybody and they all went home.

4. *Ati-azyak with his six brothers go to marry the seven daughters of the king of Lung-da.*

Now the child grew up very soon, and calling his six other brothers he said to them :—" You should not stay idle as you do, you should all work. Now we are seven brothers, and I hear the King of *Lung-da* has seven daughters, let us go and ask if we can marry them."

The *Ati-azyak-pono* gave them a great deal of gold and silver, and told them that first of all on their journey they would come to a high black mountain on the top of which they would have to place a black flag. The next mountain they would come to would be a big green one, on the top of which they would have to place a green flag. After passing that they would have to reach the summit of a red mountain where they would have to place a red flag. The last mountain they would reach would be a white one, and on that they would have to put a white flag. Then they would have to cross a table-like meadow called the *Pemo-pathong-partam*, where two suns would be shining, and where they would also find a shady fir (*chenden*), standing in the centre. Owing to the two suns, the heat would be tremendous and it would be advisable for them not to stay long in the meadow or under the fir, and they had better not take their hats off.

The six brothers started on their journey finding everything exactly as *Ati-azyak* had told them. After passing over the mountains, they came to the flat table-land where the two suns were shining, and passing through that land soon they came to the *Lungda*-palace. They showed the king all their wealth and asked if they might marry his six eldest daughters, whilst they asked for the youngest daughter whom they would give to their young brother.

The king consented to give all his daughters, and at the time of returning he told them not to play their bamboo flute (*pa-lit*) or the Jews'-harp (*tung-dyu*) as they ought not to stop long in the meadow.

But on the journey the three younger brothers with the three younger Princesses became very joyful, and started to sing and dance, so that when they came to the meadow of the two suns, they sat under the shade of the tree and felt cool. The three elder brothers with the three other Princesses and the seventh youngest Princess advised them not to stay, but as they would not listen to them, they also had to join them.

As they were all resting, they saw a big white sea approaching them from the end of the meadow where the sun rose, while a big black sea rolled towards them from the end of the meadow where the sun sank, and from the *Lho* (the Highlands) a red sea approached, and from the *Dang* (the Lowlands) came a green sea. Thus they were surrounded on all sides by water.

Out of the sea came a huge serpent towards them. His mouth was as large as a basket (*tung-jang*), his eyes were like two large cups (*tuk-chim*), his body was as large as a big rolled bamboo mat (*ta-lu-thul*), and his fins were like a flame of fire (*mi dyak*).

He asked them why they had come to his country as he was ready to devour them. They prayed for their lives and the serpent said :—"Give me your youngest brother who is at home, and then I will let you go away in peace."

This all the brothers promised him, and he then vanished with all the seas and one of the suns.

5. *Ati-azyak visits the sea-serpent.*

In the country of *Lyang-bar*, the youngest son lay in his mother's lap, and told her his brothers had been treacherous, and that someone would soon come from the Serpent-king to fetch him away. He asked her to prepare some food for the messenger, and to be sure and make some drink ('*chi*'), to have some paddy (*zo*) and to have ready some cooked meat (*man*). This was done and the messenger soon came. He proved to be a demon, and as he stood in front of the Palace he called to *Ati-azyak* asking him whether he, *Ati-azyak*, would come down, or should he come up. The boy replied as he was the messenger of a great *pono* and he was only a boy, he had better come up.

Because he was so large, the demon came in at the door with great difficulty, and sat down whilst they fed him with eight gourds of drink, eight gourds (*ta-fyep*) of '*chi*,' eight ladles of paddy, and eight big pots of meat. The demon ate every bit of this, and then the boy *Ati-azyak* was ready. He armed himself with the sword, put on his golden hat and carried his invisible cap with him, saddled his horse and rode after the demon.

Soon he met his brothers with the Princesses and the youngest Princess *Eu-ramit*, who had been promised to him. She caught hold of him passing and asked where he was going. She said whatever adventure he was going on she would like to go to, even if it were to die.

But *Ati-azyak* told her it would not be possible for her to go with him on this journey, and that she was to remain with her sisters. He gave her two rings, both golden and one having a lovely blue turquoise stone (*eu*) in it. This matched her name and he placed it on the third finger of her left hand, putting the other on the third finger of her right hand saying :—" Should they ever change places by themselves, should the blue stone go to the right hand, and the gold ring to the left, you will know that I am no more. But if they stop as they now are, I shall be alive." Then they parted, each taking opposite roads.

6. *Ati-azyak comes before the Serpent-king.*

Then *Ati-azyak* with the demon came to the Palace of the Serpent, who was named the *Paril-bu*, the demon showed him a way through a passage on his horse. He came to a tremendous opening in which there were many golden and silver *chortens and mendongs.*[1] He wondered to what place he had come, and pulling out his sword from its sheath, he began to strike off pieces of the *chortens and mendongs* The serpent began to be annoyed, for the place *Ati-azyak* found himself in was in reality the serpent's mouth, while the *chortens and mendongs* were his teeth. He thought : "I wonder what kind of food this will be!" and coughed and gurgled in his throat spitting out what he found was in his mouth.

As the *Paril-bu* spat, he blew *Ati-azyak* back with his horse over the eight mountains.[2] Once again he rode back however to the front of the Palace, and tied his horse to a fir tree. (*Chanden-kung*). This time he met a very beautiful girl, and asked her if she knew why the Serpent-king had summoned him, and where he could find him.

The beautiful girl, who was the *Paril-bu's* queen, said he had taken the wrong road, for there he would be sure to die. But *Ati-azyak* told her he had been summoned and wishing to wake the serpent up, the queen seized a hammer, and struck him from the tail to the head. He snorted and asked her why she had woke him. Telling him why, the queen called *Ati-azyak*, and the serpent told him he had been summoned so that he could go and fetch the two queens —*Zer-y-ong* and *Konyong-pandi*.

7. *Ati-azyak starts on his errand with the help of the serpent's wife.*

But the beautiful girl giving him plenty of good and sweet food that night, said to him :—" To-morrow when you go, you will meet first of all two dogs who will rush growling at you, trying to bite you, you must then give them these which will drive them away," and she handed him

---

[1] Round and oblong memorial structures that are built of stone and used by Buddhists.

[2] This huge serpent seems to be the same as the one coupled with the flood, judging by his name, *Paril-bu*. See Creation stories, p. 358.

two balls of paddy. "Passing there," she continued, "you will meet a pair of tigers who will lie in wait to spring on you. Throw this meat at them when they will turn back. Next you will meet the demon *Shang-tang-krbu* who will come to eat you. You must give him this," she said, handing him a roll of cloth (*pan-den mam-zo*), "once he receives this he will be at peace with you, and will go with you to fetch the two queens *Zer-y-ong* and *Konyong*.

Then *Ati-azyak* planted a field (*nyot*) of paddy (*zo*) before he left and said to her :—"Watch this growing, should the paddy come up you will know I am still alive, but should only weeds appear, you will know that I am dead."

When he came to the *Sari-nong-dong-chen* Pass he tied his horse up, giving him a golden and a silver ball to eat and saying :—"In five times twenty and eight years I shall return, if I am not back by then, you will know I am no longer alive."

He came next to the *Sari-rung-dong-chen* country finding the two big fierce dogs who jumped at him. However he threw them the two balls of paddy, and they turned aside. Going on he met the two tigers who were ready to spring on him, but giving these two the pieces of meat he continued on his way.

Then he met the demon called *Shang-tang-krbu*, who also tried to catch him, but *Ati-azyak* threw the roll of cloth at him saying :—"Know your master!" and at once the demon became quiet. *Ati-azyak* told the demon he was to accompany him to fetch the two Queens, so the demon put him in his pouch, and moved on.

But midway the demon took him out of his pouch saying :—"But you seem to me to be a sham sort of a master," and he tried to swallow him. *Ati-azyak* however stuck in his throat, and the demon vomited and put him back in his pouch again saying :—"After all you must be my real master as I am not able to swallow you!"

8. *Ati-azyak comes to the land of the seven demons with whom he has a contest.*

When they came to a pond, *Ati-azyak* was very thirsty and got out of the pouch to drink some of the water, but as he was drinking his knife (*ban*), fell out of its sheath into the deep end of the pond. He asked the demon to try and find the knife, but he could not, so he corked himself up and started to drink, but though he dried up the pond, the knife could not be seen anywhere.[1]

[1] As *Ati-azyak* ultimately kills him, it would be interesting to ascertain whether he is identical with the *Yong-li-pono*. See p. 358.

The demon started drinking up the streams and *Ati-azyak* went on till he reached the Palace of the queen *Zer-y-ong*, and finding her there he lived with her as her husband. He found all the streams were dry and the people were dying from the lack of water. The queen wondered what was the reason of it and *Ati-azyak* replied the drought was caused by the demon who, searching for his knife, had drunk all the streams dry. The queen said :—" Your knife was washed up here in a stream close at hand, so tell the demon to send back the water."

So the demon, after *Ati-azyak* had told him, pulled out the cork and the water rushed out and started running like a big river sweeping over a great part of the country.

Then *Ati-azyak* put the invisible cap on his head, and brought the demon to the Palace.

Now the queen had seven brothers who were all demons, but who were out hunting at that time, and the queen wanting to keep *Ati-azyak* safe, closed him in a box that was called *Samo-itmo-tang-bo* which she locked up and placed in the twelfth room of the Palace.

When the seven brothers returned they told their sister they had heard that *Ati-azyak* had come to the Palace. She was not to hide him as they would like to see him even if she would not allow them to eat him. At first *Zer-y-ong* would not listen to them, only when they still pressed her, she made them swear an oath vowing that they would not eat his flesh or drink his blood. She made them place their hands in water and the oath being so heavy dried the stream up, then secondly, she made them put their hands on a rock and the oath was so great it split the rock in twain, and then for the last time she made them swear on a sago-palm tree, and the oath was so violent it made the tree wither. After that she believed and trusted them, and going to the twelfth room of the Palace she unlocked the box and set *Ati-azyak* free.

9. *Ati-azyak plays Hide and Seek with the Seven Demons.*

So they all started living together, and as the demons, on account of their oath, could not eat *Ati-azyak* immediately, they asked him to play with them, and suggested he should seek them whilst they hid.

(*a*) *Trees.*—The next morning, the seven demons went off to hide. The queen *Zer-y-ong* gave him a knife and told him he would find seven trees in a line not far away, which he was to try and cut down. *Ati-azyak* searching for the demons later, came across seven trees all standing together in one place. These he threatened to cut down, when they all laughed, becoming the seven demon-brothers once more and saying :—

"We thought you were going to cut us down, now we had better all go home together."

As they reached the Palace the demons said:—"Now to-morrow it is your turn to hide, and we are to search for you." The next day at cock-crow, *Ati-azyak* flew up to the *Rum* country, and from *Sari-rung-dong-chen* he watched the seven demon brothers searching for him everywhere. When they found him, they said among themselves, they would chew him, and though looked well for him everywhere, even in every leaf, they returned home unsuccessful.

Ati-azyak came down and met them on the doorstep; he said he also had been unsuccessful, he had tried to find himself all day but had been unable to! At this the seven demon brothers became angry saying:—"Now to-morrow we will hide again, and you will have to seek for us."

(*b*) *Partridges.*—As soon as the cock crew, they started off and *Ati-azyak*, after feeding was ready to follow. But first of all the queen *Zer-y-ong* told him he would find the seven brothers who had turned themselves into partridges (*kohom-fo*): they would be sitting in a line. He would have to try and snare them with the horsehair snare she would give him. So *Ati-azyak* went after the footprints, noticing that sometimes they were those of animals, and sometimes those of men.

At last he came to a meadow where he saw seven partridges perched in a line on a tree. He began to spread his net around them, when they laughed at him and changed back into the seven demons. The next morning *Ati-azyak* went out to hide, and he covered himself with the feathers of a bird (the *sael-fo*).

The seven brothers searched for him thoroughly, not leaving even a stone unturned, but they could not find him. That evening *Ati-azyak* met them again on the doorstep saying:—"You could not find me and I hid myself so well that I lost myself!"

(*c*) *The Seven Streams.*—Again the seven demons went out to hide, and the queen, giving him a cup, said he would find them in the form of seven streams. "Take this with you," she said, "and where the seven streams meet, take the cup from your pouch and try to take a drink from them."

Ati-azyak acted as the queen told him, and when he tried to drink, the seven streams turned into the seven demons and they returned home together.

(*d*) *Wrestling.*—The brothers suggested they would all wrestle on the next day, and when the time came, *Ati-azyak* started wrestling with the eldest. At the third round the demon was knocked down, and *Shang-tang-krbu* seized him and pretended to swallow him. In this way all the other six brothers were defeated and *Shang-tang-krbu* pretended to swallow them in turn till at last they cried for mercy and told *Ati-azyak* to-morrow they wished to fight with cocks. He replied that as he was a stranger he hadn't a cock, and wanted to know where he could get one. The demons said :—"Well, if you haven't one, you must come after what will be your last meal."

10. *Ati-azyak contests with the demons, using fighting animals.*

(*a*) *Cocks.—Ati-azyak* then prayed to his *Rum* father and to his *Rum* mother to send him a cock, and the blind hen who had been swallowed as a hailstone and re-born, came along and laid an egg. That night it hatched, so the next morning early he found a chicken. Feeding it well he cried :—"If I am to win the fight through you, you must crow three times after you have finished your meal."

Ati-azyak's cock crew three times, but his master saw that in the playground many big cocks belonging to the demons had collected. But he came out carrying his cock under his arm, and when he set it down they all started fighting. At the first round the small cock grew bigger, at the second round it grew bigger still, while at the third round it was equal in size to all the others. *Shang-tang-krbu* picked up the other cocks as soon as they had been killed, and swallowed them one after the other.

At last the seven demons said :—"Well, to-day you have defeated us, we were very surprised to see your cock, but to-morrow we will have a goat fight. Should your goat win you may take both the *Zer-y-ong* and the *Komyong* queens, but should our goats defeat yours we will both eat your flesh and suck your blood."

Ati-azyak replied that as he was a stranger he hadn't a goat and wanted to know where he could get one. The demons said :—"Well, if you haven't one, you must come after what will be your last meal."

(*b*) *Goats.—Ati-azyak* then prayed to his *Rum* father and to his *Rum* mother to send him a goat, and the goat who had been blind in one eye, who had been swallowed as a hail stone, and re-born, came along and gave birth to a kid. *Ati-azyak* gave him a golden and silver ball to eat, telling him to bleat after eating if he were to win the fight. After feeding, the goat bleated three times, and as soon as he had brought him down to the playing-ground, he commenced fighting with all the demons' big he-goats.

The first time the small goat went round, he was a little bigger, the second time he was bigger still, and the third time he was equal in size to the other goats. Then he began to throw the other goats down which *Shang-tang-krbu* swallowed as soon as they had fallen.

The seven demons said :—"To-day we are also defeated, but don't get proud, for to-morrow we shall have a bull-fight."

Ati-azyak replied that as he was a stranger he hadn't a bull, would they lend him one of theirs? The demons answered that if he hadn't a bull, he would have to prepare to die.

(*c*) *Bulls.*—So *Ati-azyak* burnt incense and prayed the *Rum* father and mother to send him the cow who had been blind in one eye, and who had been swallowed as a hailstone to be re-born, and she came to him and gave birth to a bull-calf in the night. Giving him some grass, *Ati-azyak* said:—"After eating, and if I am to win you must low three times." And the calf lowed three times. The next morning when the demons had collected all their bulls on the playing-ground, *Ati-azyak* led his down, and the ground was shaken by their roaring.

They started fighting, and at the first round the calf started to grow, at the second round he was bigger, and at the third round he was equal in size to the other bulls. He commenced then to knock them down, and *Shang-tang-krbu* swallowed them as soon as they had fallen. But the demons said:—"You have beaten us again to-day, but to-morrow we will fight you with horses. Should your horse win, you may take the *Zer-y-ong* and *Komyong* queens, but if you lose, we will eat your flesh and suck your blood." *Ati-azyak* said once more he was a stranger and hadn't a horse, but if they were to lend him one, he would fight. The demons answered that if he hadn't a horse, he must get ready to die.

(*d*) *Horses.*—But *Ati-azyak* went home, and burnt incense and offered '*chi*' to the *Rum*, praying them to send him the mare who had been blind in one eye, and who had been swallowed as a hailstone to be re-born, and she came to him and gave birth to a foal in the night. The next morning *Ati-azyak* gave him a handful of gold and silver to eat saying:—"If I am to win, neigh after eating this food." The foal neighed three times after eating the food, and he was heard in the *Rum* country. By this time, the demons were all ready to fight with their horses and called to *Ati-azyak* to come to them at once.

Ati-azyak went down to the playing-ground taking his foal, and leaving him in a corner of the field. They all started biting and kicking each other, and at the first round the foal got larger, at the second round larger still, while at the third round he was equal in size to the other horses. He kicked so that all the other ponies began to fall down, and the moment they had fallen *Shang-tang-krbu* swallowed them. The demons said:—"again to-day you have beaten us, now to-morrow we will fight with wild bulls. (*sachak-long*).

Ati-azyak once more said he was a stranger, and hadn't a wild bull, but the demons only said:—"If you haven't a wild bull, say your last three words, and be prepared to die."

(*e*) *Wild Bulls.*—So *Ati-azyak* burnt incense, and offered '*chi*' to the *Rum* father and mother praying they would send him a wild bull.

And the next morning at sunrise he found a wild bull standing outside, so *Ati-azyak* made him ready and brought him to the fighting ground. The bulls started to fight, and at the third round *Shang-tang-krbu* pinched the bulls' necks and swallowed them. Thus *Ati-azyak's* wild bull won, but the demons said at once they would fight on the morrow with peacocks. He said again he was a stranger, and had no peacock, but the demons only said that if he hadn't one, he must prepare to die.

(*f*) *Peacocks*.—But *Ati-azyak* came back and offered incense and '*chi*' to his *Rum* father and mother, praying to them for a peacock. And they sent him a peahen at once which laid an egg, and then returned to the *Rum* country. But the egg hatched out the next morning, and he found he had a pea-chick. He asked it to cry three times if he were to win the fight that day, and to his joy, it cried three times loudly, and was heard in the *Rum* country. Soon the demons had their peacocks quite ready, and told *Ati-azyak* to bring his along quickly.

Then they commenced fighting, and at the third round the peacocks were all knocked down by *Ati-azyak's* bird and swallowed by *Shang-tang-krbu*. But the demons asked him to meet them on the next day with their army. *Ati-azyak* replied he was a stranger, and had no army to fight for him. The demons said unless he produced one he must prepare to die.

(*g*) They made ready for the morrow, but *Ati-azyak* became very sad having no one to fight with, and he lay down that night thinking hard.

Just at that moment, the pea-chick put two round stones in the fire, and when they became red-hot he called his master and told him his heart must be as strong as the stones.

Then *Ati-azyak* got up to prepare himself and made a shield and some bows and arrows. He saw the next morning the demons' army was very large and he was quite alone. The pea-chick said :—" You must fight them, but I shall be watching from the top of the house."

They commenced fighting, and *Ati-azyak* let all his arrows fly which hit all the demons, *Shang-tang-krbu* helping a lot, and at last there was only one demon left. *Ati-azyak* had struck him, but only one ear was cut off, and then he had flown away. He thought the battle was over, but the peacock said that the remaining demon had only gone to fetch several others. His master had better wait, he said, for he, the pea-chick, would go and fight them. Seeing the army advancing and led by the demon who had lost an ear, he flew to a tree close at hand which he alighted on, and asked the demon with whom he was going to fight now. They all answered :—" With *Ati-azyak* who has killed so many of our men."

The pea-chick said :—" Well, whether you kill him or not,

would you all not like to see a dance that I can show you first ? "

The demons said they would, and standing in rows, they watched the peacock who, spreading out his beautiful eye-feathered tail, commenced to dance slowly. The whole army became so interested that they watched it closely, till at last a flame of fire came out of the pea-chick's tail burning them all to ashes.

11. *Ati-azyak with the two queens starts on his return journey.*

After burning the army, the pea-chick returned to the Palace of *Zer-y-ong* and told *Ati-azyak* to go and find the queen in her room. He went in but found she had two very long tusks, one touching the sky, and the other falling down to the earth. Her breasts were so long, that one of them was thrown over her shoulder while the other hung straight down.

Ati-azyak came out again quickly and hesitated when the pea-chick asked him to go in the room once more. But he did at last, and found the queen had changed into a very pretty girl. She was so pretty that you were never weary of looking at her whichever side you looked, and you never grew tired whether you looked at her from the back, the front or the side. The pea-chick at last said :—" Now master and mistress, you must return to the *Lyang-bar* country for I must return to the country of the *Rum*."

Both the *Zer-y-ong* and *Komyong* queens prepared sufficient food to feed *Shang-tang-krbu* which they fed him with, and then they all went into the Palace, which the demon tied to his back. Hé soon came to his own house which he also strapped to his back, and when they came to the *Sari-rung-dong-chen* country where *Ati-azyak* had tied his horse up. It had been there for so many years it had sunk into the ground. *Ati-azyak* asked his horse to come out of the earth, but he replied that he could not unless he were sure that his master was there. So the queen *Zer-y-ong* sent her spinning-rod down to him which had a ring of *Ati-azyak* tied on to it, and the horse seeing his master's ring, and believing he had really come at last, sat on the rod and allowed himself to be pulled up.

Then *Shang-tang-krbu* put the horse in the Palace too with the others and carried him. They then came to the Serpent's house and found him sleeping. The Serpent-king was so long that he had curled himself up into three times twelve coils, twelve times he had curled himself up on the ground floor, twelve coils of him lay in the middle storey and twelve coils of him lay in the upper storey.

Ati-azyak pointed him out to his demon and told him the serpent was a present of food for him. *Shang-tang-krbu* was very happy and swallowed him up from the head to the tip of the tail. "To-day," he remarked, " I have really had enough food!" and taking the beautiful girl up and carrying her also on his back in the Palace they came to the country of *Lyang-bar*.

12. *Ati-azyak punishes his brothers and kills the demon.*

Once there *Ati-azyak* showed them the three younger brothers with their wives, and told him he could do what he liked with them. So the demon swallowed them one after the other. Then he was told to put *Zer-y-ong's* Palace on the side of the sunrise, *Komyong's* Palace on the side of the sunset, the Serpent-king's Palace on the *Dang* side (the Low lands, south) and his own house on the *Lho* side (the High lands, the north). *Ati-azyak* put his elder brother on the side of the sunrise, his second elder brother on the side of the sunset, his third elder brother on the south, keeping the house on the north for himself.

Then he killed *Shang-tang-krbu*, cutting off his head. The flesh he chopped up and gave to the ants while the bones were crushed by him and thrown in the air. He found the bones of some human in the stomach, and these he washed thoroughly, and wrapping them in silk he put them in a bamboo stem with a bow and arrow, and a spinning-rod, saying:—"If you are born as a boy, you will be found shooting with this bow and arrow, and if you are born as a girl you will be found spinning."

On the third day he returned to the bamboo stem and saw a lovely boy inside shooting with the bow and arrow. *Ati-azyak* went with him into his own house and inviting many people from the sunrise to the sunset, from the North and from the South, he gave them a feast and they all made merry for seven days. He asked them to suggest a name for the boy, but no one was able to, and at last he thought of a name, the *Dediong-pono*. Everyone seemed pleased with this, and giving him the Princess *Eu-ramit* of the *Lung-da* country for a bride, they became the king and queen of the *Lung-da* and the *Lyang-bar* countries.

13. *Ati-azyak returns to the Rum country.*

Ati-azyak told them that as they had no enemies and could live happily, he with his three wives, *Zer-y-ong*, *Komyong* and the queen of the *Paril-bu* would return to the *Rum* country to which he belonged. Should the clouds break as they flew upwards, it would mean they would all meet again in this world, but should the clouds cover them, it would mean they would only meet in the next world.

As they tried to fly away the others caught hold of them so that they were unable to rise. The next morning when the others were all still asleep, they managed to fly away. *Dediong* and *Eu-ramit* woke up soon after and saw them flying in the sky. Watching they saw them become the size of birds, and then they looked as small as flies, and soon were completely hidden by the clouds. *Ati-azyak's* horse who had also been let loose reached the country of the *Rum* long before the others.

Thus the country of *Lyang-bar* became free of all demons who were subdued by *Ati-azyak*.

XXVII. The Adventures of the Merchant-widow's Son.

(*Told by Shamelyangaat Toqn, May 19th.*)

1. *The merchant-widow's son receives a luminous flower.*

Once upon a time, there was a King called *Pid-no*, who had many councillors and among them were seven devils (*dut-mung*). These seven were so powerful, the King found he could not control them. *Tashey-thing* came to hear of this and made a plan to help him. In that country there was a merchant who carried trade from the plains to the coast, and back from the coast to the plains. He had a wife but no children, and *Tashey-thing* thought he would make use of this. Soon the merchant lost his life whilst travelling, and after his death, the wife had a son. Though he grew up and promised to be very strong, the woman always kept him hid, knowing the devils who really controlled the country were exceedingly cruel.

The mother worked daily in some houses and spun in others, and they both had to live on what she earned. One day as she would be out late, she made him some sour barley bread (*ka-hru-khu*). She made seven loaves which he was to eat whilst she was out, but on no account was he, she said, to leave the cottage.

But as he was playing on the balcony, a fox came to the front of the cottage, holding a beautiful flower in his mouth. The flower looked so beautiful, that the boy found he was unable to stay in the cottage, but ran out following the fox. He ran along over three mountains and saw from the ridge of the third that the fox had dropped the flower in the valley below. Reaching it, he picked it up and realized he could not return that night and his mother would be very anxious. He didn't get back till the next day with the flower he had picked up. The mother was happy to see him again, and as soon as he had brought the flower in the cottage, rays of golden light fell from it.[1] His mother told him to keep it in a safe place, but the boy said he would like the King to have it.

---

[1] Magical flowers are heard of in the folk-lore of different nations. Cf. *Golden Bough* vol. xi, pp. 45. sq. In Southern Russia it is believed that when a fern blooms on Midsummer's night, it bears a fiery flower. Whoever overcomes the dangers and plucks it will be able to find hidden treasure.

2. *The flower is presented to the king, but the councillors advise him to order the boy to bring more.*

The next day he took the flower to the King who was so delighted he called his councillors together and said :—"You are my councillors, but what have you ever done for me? Look at this boy who has just brought me this wonderful flower shedding forth such a beautiful golden light."

The *Rum* or god-like councillors said to each other:—"Alas! it is quite true, we have not done much for the King in any way," but the seven devils rose up saying:—"Yes, it is quite true, we councillors have not done much work for the King, but bringing one flower is a very little act; ask the boy to bring several so that the Palace is completely filled with them; in that case we will praise him, if he cannot, we will not praise him, rather will we think of him as an enemy."

They dispersed while the King told the boy what his councillors said, and returning home, the boy became very sad. The mother gave him some food and set out to work again as usual.

3. *A Beggar Comes who Promises to Befriend the Boy.*

As he was sitting sorrowfully in front of the cottage a beggar appeared before him to whom he could give nothing excepting the loaves of bread his mother had made for him. These he gave to the beggar who said:—"If you are in any great trouble, mind you remember me, my name is *Dub-cham*, call me."

Soon after the mother returned and asked him if he had eaten all his food. He told her a man had come begging and that he had given it all to him. Hearing this the mother was annoyed, as she had to work hard to get any food, and they were not to waste it. She was also grieved to hear the King wanted many more flowers, as the boy said he would have to find them whether he lived or died.

4. *The boy starts on his errand, and comes to the Land of the Pigeons.*

So the boy went out searching for some more flowers, and he went on and on towards the country of *Simbi-yule*, at last coming to a place where there were flocks and flocks, of pigeons, and in the very middle of them he came across a Palace where the King lived. The boy asked for shelter for the night, and the King was very pleased to see him as he had three daughters and could not find any suitable sons-in-law, and he was growing very morose.

The King asked the boy to what place he was travelling, and

he replied he was searching for some wonderful and beautiful flowers the King of his country wanted, and described them. But the King of the Pigeons told him he had much better stay for a long time with him, as he had never heard of such flowers, and did not know where he would find them. If he ever did, he was to exchange one of the golden flowers for one of his daughters. The boy hoped he would be able to find the flowers and went further on his search.

5. *He comes to the Land of the Paroquets (fari-fop).*

So he went on until he came to another country where he saw flocks and flocks of paroquets. There in the middle of the birds he came to another Palace, where the King of the Paroquets lived. The boy asked shelter from him for the night, and told him what he was searching for. The King gave him food, and told him he would find no such flower, but if he were to, after all, he could marry one of his three daughters should he like to give him, the King, one flower.

6. *He comes to the Land of the Peacocks (mung-yung).*

Then the boy left that country and came to a land where there were flocks and flocks of peacocks. In the centre of them he again found a Palace which was beautifully decorated, and as he asked for shelter, which was given him, he once more described the flowers for which he was searching. The King thought they sounded very wonderful, and promised to give him one of his daughters were he to give him one.

7. *He comes to the Sambi-ula Palace that is inhabited by five demons.*

After leaving the Peacock country the boy came near the *Sambi-ula* Palace, which he saw in the distance. But when nearer he saw it was surrounded with water, in fact it lay in the middle of an immense sea. He was unable to continue as there seemed to be no means by which he could cross, though he stayed there and thought it over for the whole of seven days and seven nights. Then he remembered the beggar had told him to call on him, *Dud-chem*, whenever he was in trouble. As soon as he had spoken *Dud-chem's* name, he felt a tremendous gust of wind which took him up and carried him to the front of the Palace where it suddenly let go and dropped him.

The flower garden, where he found himself, had many tall bushes, all of which were bearing the flowers he had been searching for so long. He also saw many other golden and silver flowers on which many golden and silver bees had settled. And coming up to the Palace, and climbing up to the lintel of the door, he hid himself in a corner.

In the evening at sunset, he heard thunder and the sound of an earthquake, and the boy saw five Evil Spirits approaching, one of whom had five heads, one three and each of the three others had two heads. They carried dead human-beings on their backs whom they were going to eat, dead horses, dead cows, and many other animals. The boy noticed with horror that the five-headed Evil Spirit was chewing the body of a young man, and as he came to the door of the Palace he ordered all the four other demons away and entered by himself. First of all he put the bodies of the creatures he had brought back with him in their different store-rooms, and sat down breathing heavily, while the boy peeping from his hiding place didn't move. Then the chief of the Evil Spirits prepared his meal, putting three human-beings in one big pot, three cows in another, and two *maunds*[1] in a third, which he ate as soon as they were cooked. When he had finished he washed himself, made his bed and dragged out a black box which lay underneath it. In a corner the boy noticed two gourds containing black and white water which were hanging up near some keys and a large black steel knife.

The Evil Spirit unlocked the box, and took out the head of a woman which he placed on the bed, adding the trunk of the body on which he placed the arms and legs. Then he watered all this from the head to the toe with the black water, and then from the toe to the head with the white water. When he had done this, the woman sneezed and came to life, and she was so beautiful she looked just like one of the golden flowers that had burst from its bud. The Evil Spirit gave her some food, and then went to sleep for the night. The next morning he once more cooked for the girl and himself, and after feeding her he made her lie down again, and poured the water from the two gourds on her skin. Then he brought out the black steel knife severing her neck from her body, also cut off the arms and legs apart. These he all put away in the box and went away after making sure it was locked. But he stealthily crept back and looked all round making sure there was no one present.

8. *The boy steals some flowers, and leaves with the maiden.*

When the demon had really gone, the boy came from his hiding-place, and opening the box, he brought the girl to life in the same way the demon had.

When the girl woke up, and saw another man she asked him where he had come from, how he had arrived, and then said it was not the place for him. The Evil Spirits were so

---

[1] A '*maund*' is roughly one hundredweight.

cruel, even birds had their wings torn off while rats always had lost their paws and nothing was ever left undestroyed. The boy told her that he had come somehow, but he wanted to know how it was he found her here. She replied :—"I was living in the *Rum*-country with my father and mother, we were just a family of three, but we had to pay revenue to the demons, one man from every house was taken, and as our house was also taxed, I was obliged to leave my father and mother and go. Here I am never able to escape as everyday they cut me up and shut me in a box, and it is only at night when the five-headed Evil Spirit is at home I am given life and set free."

The boy asked her if she would care to run away with him, and she replied if they could only escape she would go anywhere with him. He said :—"If you come with me you must not take anything with you, only the gourds of black and white water, and the black steel knife, and we ought to escape as soon as possible." As soon as he had said this they fled from the house, and picking as many of the flowers as the boy needed they came to the sea-shore.

Here the boy remembered the beggar *Dud-chem* whom he at once prayed to, and he sent them a whirlwind which carried them over to the other side. But as soon as they had arrived there the five Evil Spirits knew they had escaped and ran after them.

9. *The five demons are drowned.*

They reached the sea and started to swim to the other side, the three two-headed demons only swimming a little distance before they sank, while the one three-headed demon reached to the middle, and the five-headed Evil Spirit swam nearly across to the other side. As he came nearer, and his breath came in gasps to the shore, the trees swayed with his outgoing breath away from him towards the sunrise, and with his incoming breath they bent towards him and the sunset. In the meanwhile the whirlwind commenced blowing violently on his head, so at last he also sank, thus the five demons were all killed, so the minds of the boy and girl were easy.

10. *The boy returns home bringing the flowers.*

When these two came to the Peacock country they stayed for about a month, and at the time of his departure, the boy gave some of the flowers to the Peacock King, who gave him his second daughter. The flowers filled the Palace with gold, and the King was very happy. They came next to the Paroquet Palace and they stayed there a month. Then the boy gave the Paroquet King some of the flowers which turned everything in the Palace to gold and silver, while the King gave him his second daughter. Leaving there the four came to the Land of the Pigeons, where they stayed another month. On leaving, the boy also gave the King some of his flowers so that everything in the Palace was turned to silver, and the king gave him his second daughter.

Then the boy with the four Princesses came to his old home. He left the Princess he had obtained from the Palace of the Evil Spirits in a house they passed by the way-side, further on in another house he left the Peacock Princess, nearer his home, he left the Paroquet Princess and still nearer the Pigeon Princess, and arrived home by himself. The very next day he brought the flowers to the King, and wherever they were put, they turned everything to gold and silver, in the upper, middle and lower stories so that the King was delighted.

11. *The king orders the boy to build a palace, to decorate it, and to plant a garden.*

The next day the King summoned the councillors, and showed them all the flowers, and the wonders they had worked. The *Rum*-councillors said it was all true and wonderful, but the seven devils exclaimed they could not admit it was wonderful: the boy must at least build a three-storied Palace in three days: should he not be able to accomplish this, they said they would still think him an enemy.

The next day the boy went up to the Palace to see what the King had decided, and the King told him he would have to make a Palace in three days. The boy feeling very sad, went to the house where the Princess of the Pigeons lived, and told her what had happened. But she was pleased at the idea, and told him to rest for the following three days. Then she called up her army of pigeons who finished the Palace in three days.

On the fourth day the boy visited the King to see if he were pleased. He summoned the councillors, and asked them to admire it. The *Rum*-councillors did, but the seven devils said :—“ No, we cannot admit this is wonderful, he, your boy, must at least decorate the entire Palace (in one day) throughout with pictures of figures, animals and birds, the outside as well as the inside. Until he does this, we shall still think he is an enemy.”

When the boy understood what he had to do in one day he went in great sorrow to the Princess of the Peacocks. When he had told her what he was to do, and that he would lose his life if he failed, she told him not to worry but to rest that night, and she would order her Peacock army to ornament the Palace that very night. They flew over at once, and the army of peacocks made the Palace look gorgeous, making the whole building look like a peacock with his tail outspread.

The next day the boy again visited the King and asked him if he were pleased. The King summoned the councillors, and the *Rum*-people said it was beautiful, but the seven devils still wished for something more.

"He should be able to plant trees" they said, "or cover the table-land meadow of three fields with a forest. If the trees are there to-morrow morning, and should there be birds singing in them, we will think him wonderful, till then he is still an enemy."

This time the boy, feeling sadder than ever, went to the Princess of the Paroquets, and telling her what he had to do she said :—

"You must not grieve, I will call my paroquet army and they will work for you, only rest." The army came and planted the forest in the table-land, and the next morning as all the birds were singing the boy was sure the King would be contented. But when he went to the Palace, and the King called the councillors, though the ones from the *Rum*-country were pleased, the devils again wanted him to do something more. They said :—

12. *The boy is ordered to explain the origin of the Tista river.*

"For this alone we cannot praise him, to-morrow tell him to explain the origin of the source of the *Rung-nyo-ung* to us" (the *Tista* River).

The King repeated what the seven devils had said to the boy, who weary and sad, went to see the Beautiful Girl he had saved from the Evil Spirits. When she heard the cause of his sorrow she said :—

"Don't feel sad about this, you had better stay in the house and rest. I will go and visit the King myself."

When she reached the Palace she told the King that the boy was very young to answer such a question: he would have to die and ask his father or his grandfather in the *Rum*-country. He also would not be able to return for seven days. The King had given him a task, he had performed many difficult deeds, and the King had never rewarded him, his only recompense was to set him this hard question.

But her visit did not bring any comfort to the boy, who had to accompany her to the Palace later. She told him to pretend to be rather faint, and to say that he felt as if he were going to visit his father in the *Rum*-country.

When they reached the Palace, she spread a roll of bamboo matting (*ta-lu*) on the ground on which he lay down. She then poured the black water over him, passing it from the feet to the head, poured the white water on him, passing it from the head to his feet. She also cut off his arms and legs which she put in a basket which she carried on her back. Then she said :— "In seven days the boy will return alive, and will be able to tell you about the origin of the source of the *Rung-nyo* river.

On the seventh day the King ordered all his people to come to the Palace, everyone who could walk was to come, only the very old men, and the babies were allowed to stay at home.

As soon as they had gathered there, the girl came with the pieces of the boy who had saved her from the Evil Spirits, and she poured water on him from the two gourds in the same way she had done before, and brought him back to life. He repeated exactly what the young girl had told him to say. He said :—

"I have been to the *Rum-lyang*, and talked to my father who did not however seem to know me; he even told me I was not his son. I did not leave him at once, but followed him over many mountains so that at last he turned round and spoke to me again. He had seven brothers he said, and he would be able to tell them the origin of the source of the *Rung-nyo-ung* though he found he was unable to tell me. Then I found I was unable to follow him any further and I came back."

13. *The Seven Devils also try to visit the Rum country, but are killed.*

Then the seven devils' wives rose up and asked the King to send their husbands to the *Rum* country as they had known the boy's father all his life. To this he agreed, and on the following day before many guests, as the King had invited more people, a number of Kings and even the King of the *Lyang-bar* country with all the people who lived between the sunrise and the sunset, they copied what they had seen the girl do. The wife of each devil took a basket, a black steel knife, a gourd full of black water, and also one full of white water, and a bamboo mat which they made the devils lie down on.

They cut them up, but as they had not severed the necks in exactly the same way as the girl had done, it caused the devils much pain. They did not make any sound as no one dared cry out so they were all killed, and on the seventh day when the wives thought they would come to life, and tell the King the origin of the *Rung-nyo-ung*, they found their bodies had decomposed.

So in this way all the devil councillors were subdued, the boy took their place in King *Pid-no's* country and it became contented and happy once more.

XXVIII. How King Ling Gyaso Subdued all the Devils.

(*Told by a giggling gesticulating old woman, who intoned at Chhibo, March 10th.*)

Once upon a time in the country of the *Rum* there was a king called *Gyabu Punu*, and his Queen's name was *Thih Kiong Gyemu*. They had seven sons and seven daughters, and the youngest son's name was *Ling Gyaso.* The six brothers wanted to take the throne from their father, and they were against him and their younger brother.

At that time the whole world was filled with devils, among them being *Hore-mung*, *Kamthyong*, *Kamblyok*, and *Dut-khyung.* There were also several female demons, two of which were called *Samu-atho* and *Lhmo,* and the human-beings, being caught and eaten, suffered greatly, and they petitioned *Gyabu Punu's* youngest son to come and save them. The old king wished to send him down into the world to subdue the devils, but *Ling Gyaso* before going said:—"If I have to go down into the world, I shall need your golden bow and your golden arrows, your golden hat, with your favourite golden-coloured horse, *Tabu Chong Sey Ga-Lo*, and your favourite golden-coloured dog, *Khimo Tung-chung,* with your golden-coloured goat, *Soro-cho* and your golden-coloured cock."

And when he had started, the Queen became very sad when he reached *Siri-nong-dong-chen,* the country that lies midway between the *Rum* country and the earth, the old king heard his pony neigh, his goat bleat, his dog bark, and his cock crow, and he knew his son was leaving the *Rum* country and that all the animals would die. But they turned into grains of wheat and *Ling Gyaso* put them in his pouch.

2. *Ling Gyaso's miraculous birth.*

Soon after *Ling Gyaso* looked down on this world, and saw a woman weaving cloth in the *Ling-lyang.* Just then a fearful hail-storm arose, and the woman, a virgin called the *Imo-yout-mo-pandi* caught a hailstone, which she swallowed and gave birth to a son within a week. She found it was no child she had given birth to, but a bag tied up and sealed round the neck. At that time the king and queen were looking down from the *Rum* country on to the world to see where their son would be born. They saw the woman throw the bag on the road, where it rolled down the hill until it was stopped by a bush (the *pa-shove-nyom*) while a crow protected it from the heat of the sun and the rain.

Seeing this, the queen came down with an iron hook from the *Rum* country and asked the woman where she had put her son. The woman said she had no idea where the son was, and said she had just given birth to a bag.

Then the queen-mother looked for the bag which she found and opened with the iron hook. She saw a young male infant inside, which she gave to the woman, telling her not to throw him away.[1] "This child," she said, "will grow very quickly,

[1] So far the story is a close variant of the story of *Ati-azyak* (No. XXVI).

like a cucumber or a pumpkin. Should anyone ever ask you for him, you must never give him away, if you do I will have to come and kill you." With these words the queen left, and the woman put the child in the twelfth room of her house.

3. *The baby is given to the demons, and kills them.*

Now in that village there were two demons, who were brothers and who were called the *Afool,* and daily they used to go from house to house collecting infants for food. They heard that house had one in its twelfth room, so they came to ask for it. The woman however lied, and said she had no children, "for" she said, "I am not married and live alone."

But the demons worried her a great deal, and at last the boy came out himself and asked his mother to give him up to them; this she eventually did though she wept very much. The two brothers were pleased to get the infant, which they took away to their cottage, and put in a cooking-pot. This they covered and went away again to search for another baby.

As soon as the two demons left, *Ling Gyaso* came out of the cooking-pot, put the fire out, and seeing the many swords the demon-brothers possessed, he took one of these and hid behind the door. In the evening both the brothers returned, the elder one in front, whilst the younger was some paces behind. The younger one said :—"Don't put your hand in the cooking-pot, because we are to share equally." The eldest brother entered first, and the child jumped forward, cutting his head off so that he fell down dead, and the younger demon suffered the same fate.

Then the child set fire to the house, and returned to his mother whom he found crying over his loss, thinking he was dead. He told her he had returned, and that she was not to be sad, because he said :—"I am to be the king of this country and I had better go to my Palace."

The Palace to which he went was called the *Ling-dee,* he was made king *Ling-gyaso-gya-bo* and he married *Pamu-chi-chong-mu.*

4. *King Ling-Gyaso-gya-bo goes to the devils' country, and kills female demons and a man-eater.*

After some twelve or thirteen years he heard that a neighbouring country was much troubled by a female-devil, and told his queen she was not to leave the Palace during his absence.

He arrived at the she-devils' country and found it had a great many demons, so he disguised himself as a lama and began teaching them. After some time he said :—"I am teaching you, and you are all learning, but you ought to have a monastery, and you must build one."

They asked him what material they should use, and he advised a kind of wax (*gum or lac*), so they commenced to build and in three years the monastery was finished. He then told them he would go in and that they were to follow. When they were all inside, he told them, being a man, it was impossible for him to sit with them, as they were all women, and told them to pray while he sat near the door. When they commenced, he locked the door and set fire to the four corners of the building. One devil only out of them all, escaped. Her name was *Samu-rado lhamu* and the king followed her, catching her on the third mountain top. He brought her back and deposited her in an iron cage.

Now in the country of *Kamthyong-kamblyok* they had a man-eater, and *Ling-Gyaso-gya-bo* knew he would have to go over there and kill him. This time the queen wished to accompany him, but the king told her she was to stay at home in the Palace. The queen was very anxious to follow him, and when he started she walked behind. But soon after the King spat and a river springing from the spittle commenced to flow between them. Then he disguised himself as a fisherman and when the queen came up to him and asked whether he had seen any kings along that road, he replied he had seen no one and asked her what she was doing The queen replied she was following her husband, and he advised her not to. "Your place," he said, "is to keep the house in order, you ought not to follow your husband," and giving her some fishes he suggested she should retrace her steps.

The King then came to *Kamthyong-kamblyok*, and outside a cottage he climbed a tree and began to play a flute. The tune he played was very sweet, and the sound was heard by the wife of the man-eater. She looked hither and thither, and could see no one, but at last she found out the man in the tree was playing a flute. The moment she saw him she fell in love with him, and she asked him where he had come from and said :—"But alas! my husband is a demon, when he returns he will catch you and eat you up."[1]

The King told her he would like to be friends with her and wanted a room in her house. That evening, the demon came home making a great noise. At the same moment the king turned into a flea hiding under the quilt. He saw the demon was very angry, he had two great tusks, on one hung the dead body of a human being, and on the other the dead body of a stag. As soon as he entered, the demon said :—"I smell the blood of a human in here." But his wife an-

[1] For similar motives in this collection of tales, see above, Nos. XXV (i, 2), XXVI (6 7 8, and 9), XXVII (i). This is very common folk-lore, and is almost invariably mentioned in connection with the external soul.

swered :—"Nonsense! how silly you are, it is the smell of the human you have on one of your tusks."

In the early morning at cock-crow the demon left his cottage for his daily hunting. The king lived there for six or seven years. One day he asked the man-eater's wife if she could tell him how to kill the demon, her husband, so that he could marry her. She told him of two sago-palms close at hand, (*sa-nyol*) and of two bags of fleas. If he were to destroy these, the demon would die. *Ling-Gyaso-gya-bo* told her he would cut down the two trees whilst she boiled some water to drown the fleas. This was done, and in the evening when the demon returned with a great noise, he seemed to be ill and at midnight he died.

5. *The King returns home and kills his uncle.*

The King lived with the demon's wife for three more years, then he went home to see his own wife *Pamu-chi-chong-mu* but found *Nambo-palidung* his father's brother had sold her to a King called *Hore.* He found engraved on a shuttle which was a message from her, that he was to follow her as soon as he was able. The uncle told him his queen had been forcibly removed, and suggested, as nothing seemed to require attention in the kingdom, they should both go and trade with some country.

To this the King agreed, but wanted to know what they should take with them on their journey. The uncle told him to take some beaten rice (*tafa*) and some molasses (*garum.*)

They started on their journey, arriving at the top of a high rock where they thought they would spend the night. The uncle suggested to *Ling-Gyaso-gya-bo* that he, being the youngest, should sleep on the jagged edge. But the King, suspecting his uncle, placed the gunny bags there instead. At midnight the uncle woke up and kicked the ration bags over the edge, saying as he heard them fall :—"Now King, you are indeed dead!"

But the King replied :—"No, Uncle, here I am eating rice and molasses. What are you doing?"

The Uncle replied :—"I am not doing anything: I was only afraid you had fallen down the rock."

The next day as they had no more rations they thought they had better return home, the King thinking that although his companion was his uncle, he would have to get rid of him as he had sold his queen, and had also tried to kill him.

They returned, and on their way back they passed a flat stone which the King thought might be very useful to them. The Uncle said he would carry it if he were able to find a creeper in the jungle that would serve him as a rope.[1] However he was unable to find one and returned empty-handed. The King asked if he could take a piece of skin off his back to use as a rope, as he, the uncle had not been successful in finding any creeper in the jungle.

The Uncle agreeing, the King skinned his back, and made a rope to which he fastened the stone. This was a miracle, but as soon as the Uncle tried to have the stone up, it became heavier and heavier so that he was unable to rise, and sinking into the ground, the stone crushed him beneath it.

The King cried:—"This is no sin, for the stone killed my Uncle, not I myself."

6. *Ling-Gyaso-gya-bo goes to the country of Hore, and kills the king.*

Then the King prepared to go and fight in the country of *Hore*, leaving word with his Palace house-keeper (the *zampon*) that any letter or message he sent should be attended to at once. Then he started on his journey and when in front of the Palace in *Hore's* country, he turned himself into an infant and lay down sobbing.. The *Hore-pono* (*pono*-king) saw him thus, and taking him up in his arms thought he must be his re-incarnated nephew who had been dead these last three years. During his boyhood, the child had worked at a forge and had made swords, shields, bows and arrows. When the boy grew older, *Hore* asked him if he were his re-incarnated nephew or not. If he were, he would be able to pick out the former weapons he had made from a great many others; should he not be able to do so, it would prove he was not the re-incarnation of his nephew. Then the *Hore-pono* placed many things before him confusing his former implements with many others, but *Hore's* mother's sister told him she would change herself into a white fly, and would alight on every weapon he had made in his former life. He was to seize the implement the white fly alighted on instantly, and was to place it on one side.

Thus it became easy for him to choose, and *Hore* thought he must be his re-incarnated nephew. *Ling-Gyaso-gya-bo* also became a forger, and began to make swords, shields, bows and arrows, and he made a sword that measured the length of *Hore's* own neck, though of this *Hore* knew nothing.

Then *Ling-Gyaso-gya-bo* sent a letter to his house-keeper telling him to send two arrows in three days' time: he wanted one he had made himself, and one that the she-devil *Samu-rado-lhamu* had made of red and black iron. He wished them sent through the air. Telling *Hore* he had heard that

---

[1] The Lap-cha makes his rope from different jungle creepers including the *tane-rik*, the *kanthe-rik*, and the *tanrit-rik* (*rik*—creeper).

some enemies were coming, the army was sent with the nephew to the top of a high mountain on the third day. As soon as the army had arrived there, the two arrows flew towards the mountain top. They had become so many that the light from the sun was hidden, and everyone excepting the nephew was hit and killed. He returned to the Palace and told *Hore* the whole army had been defeated, and that he only was alive.

The next morning, the *Hore-pono* accompanied his nephew with his few remaining men, but the same fate met them, and *Hore* and his nephew were the only two that returned.

Now at midnight, when the *Hore-pono* was dozing, he heard a slight noise, and waking up asked his nephew what he was doing.

Ling-gyaso-gya-bo answered as he was feeding on rice and molasses, that he was eating his hand and arm that he had cut off from the elbow, as now being only two, they would be killed as soon as the enemy arrived. "If that be so," said *Hore*, "why not cut off my hand too, and place it in my mouth?" So *Ling-gyaso-gya-bo* took a sword and cut off one of *Hore's* hands, but instead of placing it in his mouth, he put in some rice and molasses, *Hore* saying:—"Of course it was painful but it tasted very good."

Again after a few minutes, *Ling-Gyaso-gya-bo* made a sound of eating, and the King *Hore-pono* asked him what he was doing. The nephew said:—"I am eating my foot I have cut off, as being only two we shall be killed as soon as the enemy arrives." "If that be so," said *Hore* "why not cut off my foot too and place it in my mouth?" So *Ling-Gyaso-gya-bo* took a sword and cut off one *Hore's* feet, but instead of placing it in his mouth, he put in some rice and molasses.

Again after a few minutes, *Ling-Gyaso-gya-bo* made a sound of eating and King *Hore* asked him what he was doing. The nephew said:—"I am eating my nose and my ears that I have cut off, as being only two we shall be killed as soon as the enemy arrives." "If that be so," said *Hore*, "why not cut off my nose and my ears too and place them in my mouth?"

And *Ling-Gyaso-gya-bo* thought he would now kill him, but found the knife he was holding was to small to enable him to sever his head from the body. The sword he had made to measure *Hore's* neck was jumping in and out of its sheath on the wall near by, and *Ling-Gyaso-gya-bo* invited it to come into his hand. When it came, the nephew severed *Hore's* head from his body, and whilst he was doing this, the body fought with him and the head fought with his queen, the *Pamu-chi-chong-mu*. When they had killed him, the king and queen returned to the *Ling-lyang*, but half-way home the king remembering he had left, *Hore's* son alive turned to the queen and said:—"You must return but I had better go back as I have forgotten to do something."

7. *Ling-Gyaso-gya-bo kills Hore's son.*

The King came to the palace and caught *Hore's* son in a room. He hung him head downwards, and put a plate on his head which he had filled with soft boiled rice, resting it in such a way that the mouth touched the rice. Then he found a cock which he set to fan the fire with one wing, while with the other it stirred the remaining rice; he also tied a spoon to a cat's tail and made it cook and found an ass whom he sent to draw water and two crows, a husband and a wife whom he told to fetch firewood.

8. *The King's return, and his fight with Hore's Minister.*

Then the King returned to the queen but as he was coming out of the Palace he saw a beggar. The beggar told him he was asking for alms in the country of *Hore*, and the king said to him :—" Say as you go about: The Prince is eating his food, the cat is cooking, the cock is fanning the fire, the ass is bringing water, and the two crows are fetching firewood."

By chance, the first house the beggar came to was the Minister's (the *kur-thak*), and he repeated the words the King had told him. The Minister thought as the King had been murdered perhaps his son had also met his death.

He went again to see the body of the murdered King, and saw the condition of the Prince. He and some followers rode in haste after *Ling-Gyaso-gya-bo*, and coming to a Plain lying midway between the two countries, they saw a stone which the nephew had shot an arrow into, piercing it four inches deep. Here they also found a letter which read: "Whoever comes here must look at this arrow-mark, and should he not be able to do the same, he must follow me."

The Minister noticed the arrow-mark but was only able to pierce the stone two inches, whilst all his followers failed entirely.

Then he went on alone and after some time catching up *Ling-Gyaso-gya-bo* he said :—" I have come to fight you for having killed our King and Prince." But *Ling-Gyaso-gya-bo* answered :—" If you want to fight me, it is you who must shoot first." The Minister disagreed but the king telling him he could not possibly hurt him as he wore armour, he finally agreed to aim.

Drawing his bow against the King who leant forward, he only struck the back of his horse, the arrow wounding it three inches deep.

Then the King said :—" I told you to aim at me, but you struck my horse." And cutting some flesh off the Minister's horse to fill up his own animal's wound he said: "Now it is my turn, but I cannot aim at your body because you have armour on. You had better hold a needle upright in your hand; should my arrow go through its eye I shall be the winner."

The Minister held a needle upright, and the King saw a

small space underneath his arm that the armour did not cover. Aiming at this, he killed the Minister who fell from his horse. The King mounted the dead body once more which he tied on with a weighing basket (a *tang-free*) full of powdered chillies, and striking the horse two or three times made him run into his own country. The Minister's followers were waiting on the Plain. At first they thought he had returned to them after having won. But when the horse reached them the chillies were escaping out of the bag, and the powder entering into their eyes and their noses, poisoned them so that they all died.

But *Ling-Gyaso-gya-bo* then came back to his Palace, and lived happily with his queen ever after, and this is how he subdued all the devils in the world.

D.—Varia.

XXIX. The Story of a Fool.

(1) The fool kills his own mother. (2) The elder brother wishes to cremate the body of his dead mother. (3) The fool loses her body, kills another woman, and brings her to the pyre. (4) The fool kills a lama. (5) Both brothers run away.

XXX. Hongrugm, the liar.

(1) The liar brothers try to get the orphan's silver box. (2) One of the liars enters the tomb, and pretends to be the boy's father who is speaking. (3) The liar-king is asked to divide the silver. (4) Hongrugm pretends to die. (5) Hongrugm pretends to kill his wife. (6) The two brothers kill their wives. (7) A marvellous pony. (8) The liar-king and a merchant who is thrown down a precipice. (9) Hongrugm kills the liar-brothers.

XXXI. A Tale about the *Rung-nyo* and the *Rung-nyit* Rivers.

(1) The two rivers agree to marry. (2) The two pilots. (3) The *Rung-nyit* passes the meeting place. (4) The *Rung-nyit* apologizes.

XXXII. *Ti-kung-tek, Nikong-ngal* and their bird.

(1) *Ti-kung-tek* kills the hen belonging to *Nikong-ngal.* (2) A bird in the jungle is fed by *Nikong-ngal.* (3) The ruse is discovered, but *Ti-kung-tek* hides himself in his wife's basket. (4) They settle in a hut and live on stolen cheese and honey. (5) *Ti-kung-tek* frightens the shepherd.

XXXIII. Two Sisters and a Witch.

(1) One of the sisters has an ominous dream. (2) The witch comes to take the sisters away. (3) The witch kills the elder sister, becoming a queen herself. (4) The younger sister comes to weep at the river side where her sister was drowned. (5) The witch kills the elder sister for the second time. (6) The king learns the mystery and kills the witch.

XXXIV. The King of *Lyang-bar* and the two witch nurses.

(1) The queen with her two nurses throws plates in a river and make them float. (2) The queen is frightened by the loss of a golden plate and runs away. (3) They come to the palace of the *Sachak-lat* land, the king tries

their talents. (4) The king departs, leaving two wonderful animals to bring him news. (5) A fisherman saves the children from the river. (6) The witches plot destruction of the children again. (7) The children perish but revive in a tree. (8) The king's *syce* discovers the three children. (9) The witches are punished. (10) The three children fly up to the *Rum* country.

XXXV. A Witch and her Step-daughter.
(1) A girl receives a step-mother who is a witch. (2) A fairy boy brings her food whilst she is looking after her three sheep. (3) The witch meets the fairy boy and kills him. (4) The girl finds the body of the fairy boy. (5) The girl goes to find the boy's heart.

XXXVI. The Adventures of *Duk-kung-lay*.
(1) *Duk-kung-lay* kills a tiger. (2) *Duk-kung-lay* kills a demon. (3) *Duk-kung-lay* overhears the spirits of the animals and the monsters. (4) *Duk-kung-lay* kills all the devils and witches.

XXXVII. A Tale about the *Na-ong* (the Wild Men).
(1) The woodman fells a tree, while sitting on its branches. (2) The woodman discovers his back is cold.

XXXVIII. A Tale about an Orphan Boy.
(1) The orphan boy is stolen by a tiger. (2) The orphan boy becomes king of the buffaloes. (3) A hunter compels him to marry the king of *Lung-da's* daughter. (4) A she-devil is sent to fetch the orphan boy. (5) The orphan boy returns to his shed.

XXIX. The Story of a Fool.

(Told by Sonam-richen at Kasseon. April 17th.)

1. *The fool kills his own mother.*

Once upon a time there were two brothers who lived alone with their mother as their father was dead. The youngest son only wandered carelessly about as he was a fool, and it was only the elder who helped his mother a great deal.

One day it so happened she became very ill, but the elder brother, having to go out, told his younger brother, the fool, that he was to stay in and look after her.

He agreed to do his best, and as she wanted to have a bath the fool got the water ready. But he held his mother upright and poured boiling water on her, so that it killed her instantly. As he did this, the corpse contracted making the mouth move and the fool thought his mother was smiling at him, and poured boiling water over her again.

2. *The elder brother wishes to cremate the body of his dead mother.*

When he had finished bathing her, the corpse became so stiff it wouldn't bend, so the fool tried to raise it with the help of a pair of tongs. Whilst he was doing this the elder brother returned, and pushing open the door quickly, he struck the dead body which fell.

Finding his mother was really dead, the elder brother became very upset and angry with the fool, whom he was unable to reason with.

He placed the corpse in a basket, telling the fool to carry it to the funeral pyre he was going to build.

3. *The fool loses her body, kills another woman, and brings her to the funeral pyre.*

So the elder brother started collecting wood for the fire, while the younger brother carried the basket up the hill.

But the corpse was very heavy, and the bottom of the basket gave way so that it fell out. The fool didn't notice this until he had reached the top of the hill, so he returned to find the body.

On his way down he saw an old woman feeding her fowls in front of her cottage. Seeing her he said :—" My brother has built you a funeral pyre, but you are very late," and striking her on the head, he killed her and putting her in the basket, he carried it once more to the top of the hill. The elder brother saw he had brought another corpse—not his mother's—which however he decided to burn.

4. *The fool kills a Lama.*

Thinking this, he told the fool to fetch a priest (*yuk-mun*) who would perform the service.

On his way to fetch a priest, the fool saw a wild pigeon. This he managed to kill, aiming a stone at it, and bringing it to the *lama*, asked him to follow him back for a service. The *lama* agreed to this, and asked him how he had killed the pigeon he had given him. The fool told him he would show him how he had killed it when he reached the spot where he had seen the bird.

When they got there, the fool asked the priest to stand on the spot he pointed out to him as the place where he had found the pigeon, and to coo in the way the bird had. As the priest was cooing, the fool cried :—" I struck him like this," and aiming a stone at the priest, he killed him immediately.

5. *Both the Brothers run away.*

When the fool had told this to his brother, he became alarmed and said :—" Yesterday you killed a woman, and to-day you have killed a priest. I will live with you no longer." And he ran away. But the fool ran after him carrying his grinding-stones, and when they had run some distance, they saw the priest's men following them, and as these men knew they had killed their master, they both climbed a tree and hid in the branches.

The priest's servants came to this tree, and as it was very late, they went to sleep beneath it, and the elder brother told the younger to be very quiet and said he was not to make any noise. Luckily for the brothers, the grinding stones falling down, killed all the *lama's* men at the bottom of the tree, so they both got away safely, and settled in another village far away.

XXX HONGRUGM, THE LIAR.

(*Told by Chhybo at Sindhik, May* 13*th.*)

1. *The liar brothers try to get the orphan boy's silver box.*

Once upon a time there was an orphan boy who lived near the Tibetan and Sikhim boundary. When his father and mother both died, he found he had only his father's small box of silver in the world.

Now, not far away in *Bhutan* two boys called *Haw-zemchyung* and *Paru-zemchyung* lived who were two liar brothers and these two held council wondering how they could steal the box of silver away from the orphan boy. They made a plan, and when they came near the place where the orphan boy lived, they passed the dead parents' burial place. The elder brother forced the tomb open and hid himself inside, whilst the younger brother smoothed the tomb over and made it look as if it had never been touched.

Then *Paru-zemchyung* went towards the orphan boy's house, and when he had found him he said :—" I am your elder brother, and long before his death our father told me that he would give me his box of silver."

The orphan boy said in answer :—" Father never told me there was a brother older than myself, I wonder if it is true ? "

But the liar brother replied :—" Come, let us go and ask the tomb itself if you cannot believe me."

2. *One of the liars enters the tomb, and pretends to be the boy's father who is speaking.*

So they walked to the tomb, and the orphan boy cried :— " O Father ! you never told me before your death, is it true ? Have I an elder brother ? " Then a voice from out of the tomb replied :—" Yes, he speaks the truth. You have an elder brother to whom I promised the box, you must give it to him."

They then returned towards the orphan boy's cottage, and he wept bitterly knowing he would have to give all the silver pieces up. He found the box which he gave to *Paru-zemchyung* who ran away with it at once, not even waiting to help his liar-brother out of the tomb.

Haw-zemchyung at last became suspicious, and after waiting some time, with considerable difficulty he got out of the tomb alone. Following his brother, he at last overtook him and they sat down by the wayside, and tried to share the pieces of silver equally. They tried to make a division, but as soon as each had put away his portion, he thought the other had the largest share. Some time went by, and still neither of them were satisfied.

3. *The liar-king is asked to divide the silver.*

Whilst they were arguing, the liar-king whose name was *Hongrugm,* happened to be passing. His hands were stretched across his back as he had been wetting his hair, and was now tying it up again.

The two liar-brothers asked the liar-king to divide their money for them, and he then said :—" If you want me to divide it for you, you must first of all each bring a wooden post with some rope "

They found these things which they brought to the liar-king who said :—" Now you must fix the two posts upright in the ground," and when they had done this he continued :— "Now I will tie each of you up separately, so that when I divide the money you two can't quarrel."

Then *Hongrugm* tied the two brothers up and divided the silver into two heaps. These two heaps he collected once more, and placing them in the box, he ran away with it.

The two brothers at last freed themselves from the posts and ran after the liar-king.

4. *Hongrugm pretends to die.*

Hongrugm returned to his house and told his wife two men would come and ask for him. He told her to say he had died, and they would find him lying in a coffin next door, and that she was to weep for him.

Hongrugm went in next door and lay in a coffin, holding a pair of scissors upright in his hand.

The two brothers came in, and seeing only the wife of *Hongrugm,* they asked her where he was. She replied :—" As soon as he came back he died, and he is now lying in his coffin, but if you like, go in next door and see him."

One of the liar-brothers went in to see *Hongrugm,* but as he bent down over the coffin, the liar-king cut his nose off.

But the younger brother, hiding his face purposely from his brother, told him it was quite true, *Hongrugm* was really dead, but he had better go and see for himself.

So *Haw-zemchyung* went next door, and returned with his nose cut off too. Then the liar-king laughed at them both, and said :—" Well, now you both can guess I have your silver. If you come in a week's time, you shall have it."

5. *Hongrugm pretends to kill his wife.*

The following week on the day the two brothers were coming, *Hongrugm* killed a goat, and filling the entrails with the animal's blood, he encircled them round his wife's neck, hiding them with her clothes.

When the two brothers arrived, *Hongrugm* asked them to come in and sit down telling his wife to bring '*chi*' for them to drink. Then he asked her to bring them some '*chi-sep*,' (a sandwich made of vegetables mixed with meat, chillies, salt and butter, usually taken with '*chi.*')

"But I haven't any," she cried, and *Hongrugm*, feigning anger, sprang on his wife, and cut her throat which bled terribly. She fell on the floor, pretending to be killed, and then *Hongrugm*, taking up a handful of ashes from the hearth, sprinkled them on her neck till she rose up smiling.

6. *The two brothers kill their wives.*

The two brothers were amazed when they saw him do this, forgot to ask for the return of their money, and asked for some of the wonderful ashes.

Hongrugm gave them each a handful, and they returned home. Then these two tried to do the same thing with their wives, but as they did not know of the trick about the goat, their two throats were really cut, and the wives died. The two brothers put ashes over their throats quickly, but they did not recover, and the two brothers went in anger to the liar-king.

7. *A marvellous pony.*

Outside his house they saw a pony standing on a carpet that was strewn all over with coins. When they saw this, they asked *Hongrugm* what he was going to do with it.

The liar-king answered them and said :—"This pony is always shedding coins, so I am keeping him to get more."

Then the two brothers, forgetting the past, asked for the loan of the pony for a few days. At first *Hongrugm* was reluctant, but as they continually pressed him, he at last consented to loan them the pony for a few days. He told them to feed it on vetch (*sa-lyan*) which they were to soak in salt and water. "Only" he said, "you must have a thick carpet for the coins to rest on, you will have to borrow one from a very rich man."

They followed all these instructions, and borrowed a carpet from a rich man. When they went to look at the pony the next morning, hoping to find lots of coins, they found nothing.

8. *The liar-king and a merchant who is thrown down a precipice.*

When the same thing happened the next day they went once more to the liar-king's house who said :—

"You are both, I expect, very angry with me once more, but I don't want to quarrel or to fight with you, so throw me down from a high rock in a box instead." Saying this he found a box, into which he got, and the two brothers starting to drag him walked away.

When they came to four cross roads they heard the beating of drums, the sound of which seemed to be coming from some village. The two brothers went towards the noise leaving the box on the hill. Whilst they were away, the liar-king heard some one passing. He asked him who he was and found out it was a merchant. *Hongrugm* told him were he only an ordinary mortal he had better not touch the box.

The merchant at once asked him what he was finding to do inside, and the liar-king replied that he was making gold and silver, and did not want to be disturbed.

When the merchant heard this he at once asked to be allowed inside too. He asked excitedly several times, so at length *Hongrugm* replied :—

"As you are so very eager, I will spare you a few moments," and getting out, he strapped the merchant at his own request in the box, and picking up all the merchant's goods and parcels, he returned home quickly.

When the two brothers returned they found the box in the same place, as they had left it, so they picked it up, and pulling it to the top of a rock, they threw it over. Then they ran back to the liar-king's house hoping they would find their silver. When they saw many goods and parcels outside his house, they wondered how it was he had obtained them as they had just thrown him over a rock.

9. *Hongrugm kills the liar-brothers.*

Just at that moment *Hongrugm* came out. They were very astonished and asked him how it was he had so many new treasures. He replied :—

"You did very well for me when you threw me over that rock for I found all these things at the bottom."

The two brothers immediately asked to be thrown down from the same place. After much entreaty, *Hongrugm* was at last persuaded, and carrying them to the same rock he threw them over saying :—

"You two will find much treasure down there."

After doing this he returned home, and having no more trouble with the two liar-brothers, he and his wife lived happily ever afterwards.

XXXI. A TALE ABOUT THE RUNG-NYO AND THE RUNG-NYIT RIVERS.[1]

(*Told by David Macdonald at Kalimpong, April 3rd.*)

1. *The two rivers agree to marry.*

Long, long ago the *Rong*-folk used to call the Tista river the *Rung-nyo.* He lived far away in the heights of the Himalaya mountains, but had agreed to come down and marry the *Rung-nyit* river who also lived up there, but further north. They were to meet at a point called *Dovan.*

2. *The two pilots.*

The journey was started, and the *Rung-nyit's* cicerone was a sea-serpent called *Paril Patong.* He guided her in a straight line so that she did not wander about, and came first to the meeting place. The *Rung-nyo* however had a quail (*ko-hun-fo*) to guide him, and as this quail went hither and thither in search of food the whole time causing much delay, he arrived at *Dovan* later than the *Rung-nyit.*

3. *The Rung-nyit passes the meeting place.*

So the *Rung-nyit* reaching *Dovan* first, and finding no one there, went on. When the *Rung-nyo* arrived he was very, very angry. "I am the male" he said, "and should have arrived first. The *Rung-nyit* has now passed me. I will not go on, instead I shall return the way I have come." And so speaking he turned round and flooded the whole country round for miles, and the tale of this flood is remembered by some of us *Rong*-folk to-day.

When the *Rung-nyit* heard these words she became very sad, and implored to the *Rung-nyo* be calm.

4. *The Rung-nyit apologizes.*

"A man" she said, "can also make a mistake, please forgive me, and in the future you can take your way across my shoulders."

And the Lap-cha shows how the *Rung-nyit* runs underneath the *Rung-nyo* at the place where they join. This can be noticed by the waters of the *Rung-nyo* being dark and covering completely the blue waters of the *Rung-nyit.* They also tell you to notice how straight the course of the *Rung-nyit* is in comparison with the curved bed of the Rung-nyo.

---

[1] The old Lap-cha names for the two rivers which are now known as the Tista and the Rungeet. See also another version of same story, The *Gazetteer of Sikhim*, p. 42. *Rung* is merely a prefix to all the names of Lap-cha streams, *ung-kyong* is 'river.'

And the junction of the two rivers is called to this day "*Dovan*" which means the marriage of the two rivers.

XXXII. Ti-kung-tek, Ni-kong-ngal and their Bird.

(*Told by Sadam Tshring at Kalimpong, September 8th.*)

1. *Ti-kung-tek kills the hen belonging to Ni-kong-ngal.*

Once upon a time in the old days *Ti-kung-tek* and *Ni-kong-ngal* lived in a little hut in the jungle. They had no children but they looked after a chicken. It used to run about picking up grains of rice which it gave to the Grandfather and Grandmother to live on. Although the chicken could only bring back one grain at a time, the cooking-pot was always filled, and they were both satisfied.

One day the old Grandfather said :—"Let us kill the chicken to-day and have curry." But the Grandmother said :—"But if we kill the chicken, we shall get no more rice."

Soon after, the old Grandfather and Grandmother were getting ready to go to the fields, when he said :—"You had better go on alone, as I have still some of the rice to cook."

Directly he had said this, *Ni-kong-ngal*, walked on while the old man pretended to be busy. He however killed the chicken and ate it.

When he reached *Ni-kong-ngal* again she asked him why he was so late, but he told her he had to stay a long time in the hut, as cooking the rice had given him so much trouble. When they had finished working in the fields they returned home, and though the Grandmother hunted everywhere for the chicken, she could not find it.

2. *A bird in the jungle is fed by Ni-kong-ngal.*

Then the Grandmother became very sad as she could not find the chicken, and at last the old man said :—" You must not be so sad, I know of a bird's nest in the jungle. In it there is a young bird, you must keep him instead of the chicken. Shall I bring him home for you ?" The Grandmother said :—"Yes, I do want something to look after, you must show me where the nest is."

He showed her the nest in a hollow tree but did not take her there in a straight line. Then every day, before the old Grandmother fed her bird on curry and rice, which the old man said had to be well cooked, he hid himself behind a hole in the trunk of the tree receiving all the food. At last he told her that the bird was getting so big, she would have to bring him home. After one very good last meal she cried out "Hullo!" (*Holdung*!) wanting to hear the bird speak, and the hollow trunk echoed the same word.

3. *The ruse is discovered, but Ti-kung-tek hides himself in his wife's basket.*

That day, he hid himself for the last time, and when the Grandmother cut the bark, she found the old man inside. He was laughing, but she grew very angry, and decided to stay with him no longer. So she prepared to run away and packed a great many of her things in a bamboo basket. (*tun jan*). She also packed some wine and food for her journey. *Ti-kung-tek* however hid himself under all her packages, and thinking she was well rid of him, *Ni-kong-ngal* lifted up the basket and ran over three mountain tops without stopping.

Now *Ti-kung-tek* was in the basket, and started drinking the wine he found, but a little of it leaked and the old woman stopped to look inside the basket.

Then she found the old man inside laughing at her and she abused him saying :—" You devil (*hor mung* !), I was running away from you, and now I find I have been carrying you in my basket."

4. *They settle in a hut, and live on stolen cheese and butter.*

Luckily they found an old disused hut near by where they lived. *Ti-kung-tek* used to go round stealing cheese, butter and milk every day ; some of these he brought back, but most of them he ate. One day, *Ni-kong-ngal* asked him where he found all these, and he told her that he knew where there were plenty of cattle sheds. The next day, she went with him, they found a cattle shed, and after eating a lot, they climbed up into the rafters and went to sleep.

In the evening the dairy-man returned to the cattle-shed and began to cook his evening meal. *Ti-kong-tek* said to *Ni-kong-ngal* :—" I must throw some grains of rice on to the dairy-man's head, just to amuse myself ! "

But *Ni-kong-ngal* said :—" Don't, once the dairy-man knows we are here, he will suspect us of stealing his things, and may do us harm "

5. *Ti-kung-tek frightens the shepherd.*

But the old man could not help doing it and threw some grains of rice on to the dairy-man's head. He became very frightened and thought a devil (*mung*) was in the shed, and went away to tell a *Mun* (the Rong-folk female exorcist), all about it.

The *Mun*, who was a monkey, told the dairy-man she could kill the demon were she to poke it with her tail. The dairy-man showed her the place from where the grains of rice had come, and the monkey standing on her head put up her tail through a crack in the rafters. But *Ti-kung-tek* caught hold of the tail and by pulling very hard he managed to pull it off.

So she screamed to the dairy-man, "There is a dangerous demon up here, it would be best if you were to run away."

At the same moment *Ti-kung-tek* jumped down and ran over the dairy-man who ran away all the faster being extremely frightened.

So after all this *Ti-kung-tek* and *Ni-kong-ngal* became the owners of the cattle-shed and lived happily ever after.

XXXIII. Two Sisters and a Witch.

(*Told by Din-lok at Sindhik, May 15th*)

1. *One of the sisters has an ominous dream.*

Once upon a time there were two fairies, (*khandromo*), sisters who were called *Kom-tar-hep* and *Zer-tar-hep.*. They were the keepers of a *Rum's* flower garden, and all their days were spent very happily. One night as they were sleeping on their gold and silver pillows, the youngest sister dreamt a dream. A witch had come and had taken away their pillows, her name was *Tan-gap.* She woke with a start and told the dream to her sister, and said :—"Some days are coming for us." But *Kom-tar-hep* told her not to place too much faith in dreams.

2. *The witch comes to take the sisters away.*

But *Tan-gap* really came at sunrise the next morning, and told the sisters she had come to take them away and to make them both the king of *Lyang-bar's* two queens.

The two sisters said they were not worthy to be queens, but the witch told them that if they were not willing to come she would have to take them by force. Knowing they were helpless, *Kom-tar-hep* and *Zertarhep* did their best to please the witch. They gave her eight baskets of rice, two big bamboo vessels full of *chi,* and two whole bullocks. The witch ate all this and said :—"If this is my morning and evening meal, it is not enough, but for a little refreshment only it will do."

After eating she again pressed the sisters to go with her, but they said they were obliged to sow their fields before they left, and they also had to finish their weaving.

But the witch said :—"But I can finish that at once for you," and setting to work she soon finished their sowing and their weaving.

Directly the two sisters saw her do this, they had no more excuses, and the witch told them to wear their best clothes with all their jewelry and sent them on ahead.

3. *The witch kills the elder sister, becoming a queen herself.*

They went towards the sunset and came to the *Lyang-bar* country where they saw the palace, but the witch said to them :—

"Before entering you must bathe." She brought them to the *Gyamchho-chhimo* river where she told them to take their clothes off. Then she took the elder sister down to the water's edge, cut off her head with a curved knife, and threw her in. Then she returned to the youngest sister, but *Zer-tar-hep* prayed and implored her not to harm her saying "You had better take the place of my sister, and become queen, only leave me alone for I will never breathe a word about to-day."

The witch did not kill her, and wearing *Kom-tar-hep's* clothes and ornaments, and changing all her clothes for those of *Zertarhep* they went on together towards the palace, *Zertarhep* pretending she was merely an attendant.

The king of *Lyang-bar* was greatly puzzled, but he made both of them queens, the witch telling *Kom-tar-hep* she was to feed the fowls and pigs every morning and evening. During the day she was to take the sheep out grazing.

After some time the witch became fruitful so that the king of *Lyang-bar* went into seclusion.

4. *The younger sister comes to weep at the river where the sister was drowned.*

Zer-tar-hep took her food every day to the bank where her sister had been murdered. Every day she would sit down whilst she wove, weeping and wailing. One day she gazed down into the water, and seeing her sister weaving, a tear of hers fell on her sister's loom.

Kom-tar-hep looked up seeing her sister on the bank. She came up to her, bringing many rich foods. Sitting on the bank till sun set they talked together like olden times. Then *Kom-tar-hep* had to return to her river, whilst *Zer-tar-hep* had to go back with her sheep, but by mistake she took a piece of meat back with her in her pouch. She came back as usual to the palace, the witch coming out as she always did, pretending to count the sheep, whilst in reality she devoured one whole. This she did every morning and every evening. After putting the sheep away, *Zer-tar-hep* dusted the palace. Whilst she was doing this, the meat fell out of her pouch, the witch noticing it.

The following day, the witch told *Zer-tar-hep* to stay at home looking after her child, *San-dyong-katun,* who was a giant spider.

5. *The witch kills the elder sister a second time.*

The witch came with the sheep to the bank of the river watching for *Kom-tar-hep.* When she came out, *Kom-tar-hep* thought it was her sister. She asked:—"Are the king and the queen happy together?" The witch answered that they were, and seizing hold of *Kom-tar hep*, she cut off her head once more throwing it into the river.

Then she returned with the sheep, devouring one whole as usual.

The next day *Zer-tar-hep* went out with the sheep again going down to the bank and weeping, but her sister did not appear.

Later on in the day she looked into the water again, saw her sister, noticing she had grown very large, so large, that though she sat before her loom, she could not use it.

Again she could not restrain her grief, and a tear falling on to the loom made *Kom-tar-hep* look up and sit on the bank. Once more she asked about the king and queen. *Zer-tar-hep* told them they were not as happy as they had been, as they were never together. At sunset the two sisters had to separate.

6. *The King learns the mystery and kills the witch.*

Seeing that *Zer-tar-hep* was always very sorrowful, the king asked her one day what the reason of her grief was. At first she would not reply, but when the king pressed her she told him everything.

The king told her he would alter everything, and when the witch went out with the sheep the next day, he killed and cooked the spider son, giving it to her for supper when she came home. He had also prepared a pit full of spears for her, which he had covered with a rug, telling her to sit on it. As the witch tried to sit on it, she fell on the spears which pierced her to death. At that very moment the King separated her head from her body, chopping up the flesh which he gave to the birds, and ground up the bones which he threw in the air.

XXXIV. The King of Lyang-bar and the two Witch Nurses.

(Told by Mail-li at Tumun, December 2nd.)

1. *The Queen with her two nurses throws plates in a river to make them float.*

Once upon a time, the King of *Lyang-bar's* Queen had two nurses. But both of them were really witches and wished to take the place of the Queen when they had killed her. They told her she should keep herself spotlessly clean, and advised her to bathe in the *Jam-chi-chume-der* which is a sea. When they reached the water's edge and the Queen bathed, they played with two wooden plates the nurses had brought with them, filling them with flowers, and throwing them into the water and making them float. The witches told the Queen she should bring her golden plate to play with, as that would dance on the waters still more. So, one day she brought it, and, filling it with white flowers, she threw it on to the waves, where however, it sank at once.

2. *The Queen is frightened by the loss of a golden plate and runs away.*

The Queen was very frightened, and thought that the king would be so angry that she had better not return to the Palace. The two witches fetched the Queen's horse, and they all three mounted it, the eldest witch sitting in front near its head, the youngest witch in the middle of its back, while the Queen sat near the horse's tail. They came to a land in the East called the *Sachak-lat*, and the King of that land dreamt that his future wife was coming towards him, and as he woke and looked out, he saw the three women approaching him from the *Pamen-potang* plain. So, taking up his stick, to which he had tied many coloured strands of silk, he threw it towards the horse, thinking it would fall on his future wife's back. It came straight towards the queen, and rested on her shoulders. The two witches were very annoyed, and pulling it off her back, it was taken by the eldest witch.

3. *They come to the palace of the Sachak-lat land, and the King tries their talents.*

When they came to the palace, the King told them to stay outside in one of the buildings and on the next day, he asked the eldest witch to come up to his palace. He wished to test her, and told her to wash his head and brush his hair. This she did in such a hard manner that sores came out all over his head. The King then asked her what she would like to eat and drink. She chose a pot of tea and some millet seed to soak in it. Soon after the youngest witch came. She brushed his head in just the same way as her sister had done, so that blood came out of it, and as refreshment she had like her sister, a pot of tea and some millet seed. The King then sent for the third girl, but the two witches were very angry at her being sent for, and beat her. She went there later however, and making some hot water, washed and brushed the King's hair so nicely, and pressed his head in such a soft way that he was pleased with her. Then she had some tea and dipped roasted ground rice in it, but she was so shy that she brought it down to the stables to eat. The two witches were angry at her having such good food and beat her once more. The Queen was fruitful also, and this infuriated the two witches who pretended to be pregnant also

4. *The King departs, leaving two wonderful animals to bring him news.*

The King left the palace to buy some things and told his three wives to stay at home with the puppy who was expecting young. Before leaving he tied a horse up outside the door, saying that it was to neigh should the eldest witch give birth to a son, while on the roof he placed a cock, telling him it was to crow loudly were the youngest witch to give birth to a son, while he put a flute near the bed of the Queen, telling it to blow if the Queen gave birth to a son. After two weeks, the Queen gave birth to three sons, and the dog gave birth to three puppies. The horse neighed, the cock crew and the flute sounded, but the two witches hid the Queen's children in a box, which they placed above the door of her room.

The King came back soon after he had heard the sound of the horse neighing, the cock crowing and the flute blowing, and as he came in by the door, the three children tried to catch his head. The King however was so intent on seeing the Queen again, that he did not notice them, and went straight up to her bed. When he saw the three puppies he grew very sad, whilst the two witches, fearing lest he should find the box, buried it. In anger, the King dashed the three puppies to the ground, slashed the horse, killed the cock, and broke the flute. The two witches thought that were they to keep the box buried too near the house, the King might hear the babies' cries, and threw it in a river close at hand.

5. *A fisherman saves the children from the river.*

Two old people lived near the river, having only the fish to eat which they caught. One day, these two found the wooden box which they brought home in great excitement. The old man wanted to open it at once, but the old woman advised him not to as there might be a dead body inside. However he persisted in opening it, and found three children inside, a girl and two boys. Being alarmed, they thought of throwing the box away again, but the children implored them to let them live and stay with them. They told them they would cut wood for them, fetch water and reap their fields. The two old people agreed, and from that day, they found they had always plenty to eat, plenty to wear, and lots of jewelry.

One day the eldest son said he was tired having nothing to do, and asked the Grandfather to make him a wooden horse to play with. When he had made it for them, they sat on it like the three women had, one of them being their mother—when they rode to the *Sachak-lat*. The eldest sat in front, the next sat in the middle, while the youngest sat near its tail.

One day they went to the lake on whose waters the Queen

had thrown the golden plate, and said to their rocking-horse : -- "Wooden horse, drink, wooden horse, drink." The Queen and the two witches were again bathing there, and the eldest witch turned round and said :—"But can a wooden horse drink water ?" The little boy answered :—" Can a human person give birth to three puppies ? My mother bore us, but you hid us and pretended she had given birth to three puppies."

6. *The witches plot destruction of the children again.*

When the boy had spoken, the two witches became very ill and lay down, while the Queen was very pleased at finding her children once more. The King was worried over the illness of two of his wives, and looked in his religious book to find what he should do to cure them. The two witches told him that not far away he would find three babies, if he were only to kill them and give them as food to his two wives, they would recover immediately.

The King said that, if only they would get well at once, he would kill the three children.

Now these three babies dreamt what was going to happen to them, and telling the two old people to kill the King's dog and to give him its flesh to eat, saying it was their's, they ran away.

The King took this flesh home to his wives (which he had obtained from the old people near the river) which they roasted and ate, saying after, that they had quite recovered.

7. *The children perish, but revive in a tree.*

The three children thought they had better separate, one of them took the lower road, one of them the higher, and the youngest took the middle way. After one week, the elder brother thought he had better look for his other brother and sister to see if they were safe, and wandering about he found his brother's hands and feet, and guessed an alligator had come up out of the river and had eaten him up. He also found the bones of his sister, whom he could tell a tiger had demolished. Night came, and being alone, he felt very frightened, and praying to the *Rum*, he made a fire to burn his brother's and sister's bones. Losing his balance, he fell into the flames and was burnt to death.

And in three days' time, a pine-tree sprang up on the place where the fire had been ; it grew quite big, and on it the three children were re-born.

8. *The king's syce discovers the three children.*

Now the King's *syce* thought he might find the three children, and as he was cutting grass near the pine-tree one day, he was very startled to hear it speak, and stayed there many hours. Then he went up to the palace and told the King, who however was rather angry, thinking the *syce* had lied, and sent his trusty servant. Coming to the tree the servant could see nothing though he heard voices. He told the King he had heard voices and thought the three children had been re-born in the pine-tree. Then the King visited the tree himself, but the children were frightened at his arrival and hid themselves in the trunk and would not come down. The King grew so angry, he seized his sword and tried to cut the tree down, but it proved to be like iron, and he could make no mark on it. Then he brought a blacksmith and threatened to burn it down, but it would not catch fire as water came out of the trunk and put the fire out.

Then he looked in his book once more, and found that he was to come to the tree with many *lamas* who were to say a great many prayers, and give many offerings of flowers. Were he to do this he would be allowed to see his children again.

And on the day the prayers were to be said the two witches were locked up in the iron room, and the King came with the Queen to the fir-tree. The moment the children saw their mother had come to fetch them they climbed up the tree trunk again, thinking the two witches would try and kill them. But the mother cried :—" If you are really my children, you would come down to me." Then they spoke to her and said they wouldn't come down till they had both promised to kill the two witches. They told her that these two had killed them and had put the three puppies to her breast. And as the children were telling their story the two witches heard them, and shook the palace in their anger as they thought they were safe having killed the three children again.

9. *The witches are punished.*

The King told his men to dig a big hole, telling the two witches he was going to give a great feast and would invite many guests. When they had dug the hole, the King placed many spears in it, and putting a carpet on a light bamboo fence over it, he called the two witches out to the feast. A servant showed them to the carpet, which they sat on, falling at once on to the spears which pierced them. They screamed for mercy, but the three children ran up and covered them with stones, telling them that they were only suffering now as they had made them suffer in the past. They told them that their mother had been the King of *Lyang-bar's* Queen, and that they had only been her two nurses. It was they who had made her bathe and who were the cause of her losing the golden plate which had caused so much trouble. They had not given birth to anyone, and it was they who had pretended their mother had had three puppies. It was through them they had been placed in a box, and killed, they had caused much unhappiness as they had had to run away to die and had had to be re-born. And then as the two witches were feeling thirsty and asked for some water, they poured hot ashes down their throat, and told them that was the only way they would have their thirst quenched. So these two at last died and the three children and the King and Queen made merry, all the *lamas* said prayers, and music sounded.

10. *The three children fly up to the Rum country.*

The following day, the three children said they would have to go away to the *Rum* country, but the parents were sorrowful, and asked them who would feed and look after them if they now went away. They said that they had become unclean through the puppies having been put in their place, and that now they would have to go and join the *Rum*. But before they went, they gave both the parents plenty of food to eat, clothes to wear, goats to milk and horses to ride. Then they came out of the palace, but the parents would not let them leave, holding on to their hair and their clothes. They cut themselves loose however, and flew up the Heavens, first telling both parents to watch them as they flew up. Should clouds cover them, they would never meet again, but should they be seen up to the last, they would meet on earth once more. But as soon as they were high up, thick clouds came and covered them, so the parents knew that they would meet no more on this earth, and wept bitterly. But after the space of three days, the King and Queen lived happily until the end of their lives.

Thus ends the story, the *mung* is dead, but the hero and the heroine are still alive.[1]

Told by *Mail-li* at *Tumun.* December 2nd.

XXXV.—A Witch and her Step-Daughter.

(*Told by Mail-li at Tumun, December 3rd.*)

1. *A girl receives a step-mother who is a witch.*

Once upon a time, there was a husband and wife who had only one daughter. The mother was so ill that she could not live, and yet she was unable to die. The husband told her he would be very kind to their daughter, and that he would never beat her or say unkind words to her so that she should die in comfort. This she did, the daughter of four years old weeping bitterly when the father took her down the hill to bury her.

---

[1] A parallel to No. XXIV. "*Golden Knife and the Silver Knife*".

As he buried her, he heard a little thunder from the west, and a witch followed him home, hoping she would become his wife. One of her breasts was hanging on the ground, whilst the other was flung over her shoulder, half her hair was plaited and the other half was loose. The father went slowly, and the witch arrived at the hut first. She sat down and ate charcoal from the hearth which she also gave to the baby-girl. The baby-girl still wept and would not eat this, though the witch pretended to be her aunt and filled a gourd with charcoal she wished her brother-in-law to eat.

When the father returned, he wrapped his daughter up in a blanket and put her in the opposite corner to sleep.

The witch found she was going to be fruitful and in three days the child was born. This one she fed properly leaving the other little daughter half-starved, and she became thin. The witch's child had rice but the other one only had the paddy-flower. She got still angrier with the other daughter saying her child was thin with her rice, and told the step-daughter to go and look after the three sheep. This daughter took them early far away to the Paim plains and the sheep started to graze, while the child sat down and cried.

2. *A fairy boy brings her food whilst she is looking after her three sheep.*

At mid-day she was still crying, when a boy approached her from the east, carrying a white handkerchief which he had put food in. The orphan-boy came to her saying :—"You must be very unhappy, probably you are an orphan and they have given you nothing to eat, see what delightful stuff I have brought you." And in the parcel the girl found hot tea, chicken, meat, and rice. After they had eaten, they hunted for lice in each other's head and when evening came, they separated, the boy going towards the east, while the girl brought the sheep back home again to the west.

And the boy met her every day, so with all his good food, she got fat. Seeing this the witch become angry and said at last that she would come with her to watch her grazing the sheep.

3. *The witch meets the fairy boy and kills him.*

And though the girl tried to put her off and told her it was too far away, she dressed herself up in her clothes and took a reed with her that was like the one "*chi*" is sucked up through—only it was made of iron. (*pa-hip.*)

She was also thinking she would get good food to eat and saw the boy coming towards her carrying a basket. He came nearer to her and looking hard he noticed it was not the same girl he had seen yesterday. He didn't wish to give her the basket, but the girl said she felt very hungry, and though he didn't want to go near her, she seized his hand and pulled him towards her, and looked in his head and killed the lice.

She found out his name was the *Lee-pono-kup* (which means the *boy-king*), and whilst he was asleep on her lap, she pulled out the iron reed and putting it through his ear, drove it right through his head He woke up with the pain, and moving slowly managed to get away.

That evening the witch returned with the three sheep saying to the girl :—"From to-day you can take your sheep again, and you shall have your wonderful food once more, and your '*chi*,'" and she made the little girl cry who went to bed praying for the morning.

4. *The girl finds the body of the fairy boy.*

But when she reached the plain, she found lots of blood on the place where they had sat down. She followed the traces of it which led her to a cave, and in it she found the boy lying dead.

The next morning she had a baby and she wrapped him in the boy's clothes and stayed in the cave. But at midnight his spirit appeared to her, and told her to give him back his clothes for he was cold. She implored the spirit to let her keep them as she had made them into wrappings for her child, and then the spirit went away. The next night, the spirit came and asked her for his sword, but that she also asked him to let her keep as it was under the baby's head, and she could not take it away. And on the third night the spirit came again asking for his shirt, and as he spoke, the girl got up to seize him, but the spirit implored her not to touch him as his time to return had not yet come.

5. *The girl goes to find the boy's heart.*

The spirit then told her if she really wanted him back she would find his heart with the *Rot mung* which she would have to fetch. On the way the spirit told her she would meet many tigers who would all try to devour her. After, she would meet thousands of fleas who would try and smother her by swarming all over her, and then several leeches would try and attack her by biting her. Then she would meet an old man and woman who would have no clothes on, but only pieces of stuff which they had joined roughly, having used only their fingers as they had no needle. This she was to supply them with. So in order to drive away the tigers she took one maund of meat with her, some chilli powder to drive away the fleas, and one basket of ashes to send the leeches away. She also carried a large needle.

After passing all these dangers, she reached the mango tree on which all the hearts of the dead hung, in the *Rot-mung* country. The devils used to feed on these hearts, but it was quite easy for her to distinguish her boy's, as it was still quite fresh and young, as he was to be born again. When she left with the old man and woman behind her, the leeches, the fleas and the tigers all ran after her. But she managed to reach a bridge safely which the old man and woman cut (it was only a bamboo one) directly after she had crossed.

Very pleased and tired the girl found her way back to the cave. She placed the dead heart on the dead body and went to sleep with her baby.

At midnight, the spirit began talking to her. He told her to be careful not to touch him, but as she had now brought his heart back there would be a tremendous noise. "The earth will rise and touch the sky" he said, "and some miles away, the sky will come down and touch the earth, but you must lie down quietly and not be alarmed."

During the night there was a tremendous noise but the girl did not move, and when all was quiet she went to sleep again.

In the morning, she woke up to find she was in a castle; a great many people were waiting to see the *Lee-pono-kup* and outside herself she saw lots of horses, bullocks and goats that were all hers, and everybody was surprised to see the little orphan girl in such a building and covered, as she was, with jewelry.

For six days they had a great feast and lived happily together ever afterwards.

XXXVI. The Adventures of Duk-kung-lay.

(*Told by Tuk-ten at Tumun, November 29th.*)

1. *Duk-kung-lay kills a tiger.*

Once upon a time there was a husband and wife. Now the husband was very lazy, and would never leave his bed early. One morning his wife told him to get up and see how the earth was getting on, but he did not move, and at last the wife took a pot of cream to lure him out of bed with. A jackal came to steal the cream, and the husband seeing this was so annoyed that he jumped out of bed and swallowed the cream. Then he thought he would try and catch the jackal who had been stealing lots of people's things and hiding them in a hole, and went on and on.

He stopped near a place where a tiger had been killing and eating many human-beings. He came across a woman and a child who were weeping, as they said the tiger would soon come to eat them up in their turn. But *Duk-kung-lay* told them not to be frightened as if they would only follow him he would look after them. Then he covered up all their cloth, and as he was doing this, the tiger came and carried him away with the cloth. The tiger ran until he came to a big wood where he couldn't go so fast. At last the man managed to catch his tail which he pulled so hard that the tiger ran away leaving it in his hands and soon after died. So at last everyone was left in peace.

2. *Duk-kung-lay kills a demon.*

But *Duk-kung-lay* went on further still and came across another woman with her child weeping. He asked them why they were crying, and they told him that a *dut* who had three heads was coming to eat them that night. *Duk-kung-lay* told them nothing would happen to them as long as he remained, and asked her if she kept any pigs. She answered that she did, and gave him one. This he roasted and slept near the fire which was cooking it. The *dut* came out at night to look for people whom he could eat, and stumbled across *Duk-kung-lay* who told him that he was an ogre and gave him some pork to eat. As he was munching this, *Duk-kung-lay* hit him with a burning stick knocking off two of the heads and there was only the one left. Through fear, the *dut* ran away and falling over a precipice, he killed himself. *Duk-kung-lay* came back and told the woman, and said she was not to be frightened any more.

3. *Duk-kung-lay overhears the spirits of the animals and the monsters.*

And *Duk-kung-lay* came to another country, and in it were all the spirits of those who had gone away from the earth. The jackal's spirit was there, the one who had stolen the cream, the tiger's spirit was there whose tail he had pulled off, and the spirit of the *dut* was there, whose heads he had cut off. And they were all talking together so that *Duk-kung-lay* overheard what each one said. The jackal said :—" If *Duk-kung-lay* comes let us run away. He chased me until I died from fatigue." The tiger said :—" Yes, we won't speak to him, for he pulled my tail off and I died." And the *dut* said :—" No, we won't meet him, for he struck my two heads off."

Duk-kung-lay hearing this thought he would catch them again, but they disappeared, so he couldn't. Then he went on again until he came to a devils' and witches' monastery (*dut* and *mung*).

4. *Duk-kung-lay kills all the devils and witches.*

Going in, he found one devil sitting at the table, and there were plenty of *mung*-slaves. One devil was bringing a human whom he had killed, hitting it with an iron hammer, and he threw it on to a heap of other corpses. Every day they added to the heap. They asked *Duk-kung-lay* why he had come, and he replied that it was to worship, so they told him to sit down. This he did, hiding the devil next him in a basket, whom he managed to kill with a hammer that was lying about, and then threw him on to the heap. In this way he managed to kill all the devils and witches in that monastery, and was eventually quite alone.

Then he went to *Tab-sang*, where the *Rum*, the good spirits, were fighting the devils. *Duk-kung-lay* helped them kill the devils too, and then he went to fairy-land, where they kept him for a time, though he thought he ought to be returning to his wife. He told all the fairies he had been killing jackals, tigers and devils, but found he had no work there. So he went to sleep, and when he woke up, found he was at home again.

XXXVII. A Tale About the Na-ong (the Wild Men).

(*Told by David Macdonald at Kalimpong, April 4th.*)

1. *The woodman fells a tree while sitting on its branches.*

Once upon a time a man was walking along a road when he saw a woodman felling a tree, whilst he was sitting on its topmost branches. He advised him to cut the tree down standing on the ground, otherwise when the tree fell, he would fall on the ground hurting himself.

When he had gone some distance, he heard the woodman calling him back who said :—"You must be a great teacher: what you prophesied has come to pass, the tree fell, and falling with it I hurt myself. Cannot you tell me whether I shall know when I am going to die?"

The traveller said :—"You must always feel your back; whenever you find it cold, you will know your last hour is approaching."

The woodman continued working, and finding one day that his knife (*bɔn*) was blunt, he went to the blacksmith, and sitting on a stone, watched him most of the day sharpening it.

2. *The woodman discovers his back is cold.*

When he was leaving with the sharpened knife, he felt his back, discovering it was cold. Thinking he would be sure to die, and as he passed four cross roads, he dug a hole, burying himself up to the neck in it.

Many folk passed that way, and nearly all asked him where

the different roads led to. He answered :—" Now I cannot tell you, when I was alive I knew where all the roads led to, but now that I am dead I have forgotten."

The passers-by thought it was a resuscitated corpse (*rolung*) into which an evil spirit had entered. Should he but stretch out a finger, they would all die. They consulted together, and decided they had better kill him. So drawing together, they stoned him until he died.

XXXVIII.—A Tale About an Orphan Boy.

(*Told by Kazem at the Ling-them monastery, May 9th.*)

1. *The orphan boy is stolen by a tiger.*

Once upon a time there was an orphan boy who was called *Ryothub-sang*. As he had no home of his own he lived with his brother and sister-in-law who did not care for him and never looked after him. In fact they looked on him with hatred and aversion, and he had to lie in the corner of their hut where the rubbish (*muk*) was kept.

As he was lying there one day, feeling morose and sad, a tiger came along, and picking him up, carried him away till he reached the foot of a mountain. There as he felt he would like to eat him, he placed the bundle on the ground but discovered he was holding some clothes only, the boy having slipped out of them a long way back. The tiger retraced his steps and began searching for him.

When he had escaped, the boy walked on and on towards the sunrise finding at last a cowshed. He did not see any herdsman, only noticing cows and calves, but finding much butter and cheese and feeling very hungry he sat until he was satisfied. After he thought he would clean the shed climbing up when he had finished on to a tree-fern that was growing outside, and fell asleep.

2. *The orphan boy becomes king of the buffaloes.*

At sunset he heard the bullocks returning, and noticed they had very long horns. These noticed the shed had been swept, found both the bread and butter had been eaten and as they followed the foot-prints to the tree-fern they discovered the boy asleep on the top, whilst a tiger crouched at the bottom ready to spring up at him. The bullocks at once rushed on the tiger, pinning him to the trunk of the tree till his entrails stuck on to their horns. Then they made steps up the trunk of the tree asking the boy to climb down. He was so frightened that the tree-fern shook from his body trembling. But the bullocks insisted on carrying him on their horns to the shed. Once there they asked him to be their master crying :—" Up to now no one has ever looked after us, you must be our king." They handed him a pair of golden flutes with a pair of bamboo ones, telling him that when he was in any difficulty, he was to blow the golden ones, when they would know by the sound he was in danger, but should they only hear the sound of the bamboo flutes, they would know he was but whiling away the time·

3. *A hunter compels him to marry the King of Lung-da's daughter.*

Every day the herd went out grazing, leaving the boy alone in the shed, and one day, a hunter (*sharabu*) came from the *Lung-da* country, finding the boy whom he at once thought a rich man. The hunter spoke to him, wanting him to go to the *Lung-da* country. The King there, he said, had a daughter, who had only drunk three times from her mother's breast, and had then been placed in a dark room: would he not be able to try and see her ? But the boy did not want to leave his cowshed, and when the hunter tried to take him away by force, blew on his golden horns, and at the sound all the bullocks came running together lowing. The hunter was alarmed, returning to the *Lung-da* country. Finding the king he told him that he had met a wonderful Prince far away. He had tried to take him away by force, but he had blown upon a pair of golden horns, a herd of bullocks coming to his rescue. Terrified he had come home, but he wished to tell the king that he had found a suitable Prince for the Princess.

This news pleased the king who called his diviners asking them how he could obtain the Prince for a son-in-law.

4. *A she-devil is sent to fetch the orphan boy.*

The diviners could not foretell anything, but at last they discovered a maid in the palace who was a she-devil. She told them that if they promised her a reward she would procure the Prince. They gave her a good feed, so turning herself into a crow, she flew to the cowshed, hopping from post to post cawing.

This annoyed the orphan boy who threw burning sticks out of the fire at her, failing to hit her however as she always flew away in time. At last he had nothing within reach but the hearthstones (the *gya-pu-pom*), he flung these, and then in desperation threw the golden flutes at her. These the crow picked up, returning with them to the *Lung-da* country. She showed them to the king, telling him to send men to fetch the Prince whom they would find in a cowshed.

The king sent a party of men off, who discovering the shed, surrounded it catching the orphan boy. He played his bamboo flutes wildly, but the sound only meant he was amusing himself, and the bullocks did not return.

The *Lung-da* men dragged him down to the palace, and the king shut him up in the dark room in the 12th layer of the wall, where his daughter had been kept, and closed and locked the door.

Now hours, days, weeks, months and years passed by, but the bullocks had no news of their master.

5. *The orphan boy returns to his shed.*

Now the shed lay in the jungle, and a bullock called *Thage*, who had not seen his master for 20 years, thought he would return and visit him again. Feeling sad and neglected, not finding him, he determined to stay near the shed until his master returned, but he waited so long that he sank in the ground, at length only his mouth and the ends of his long horns showing.

Then one day, *Ryothub-sang* found his golden horns and started back to his cowshed once more. He found *Thage*, the bullock who was buried and told him how a hunter from *Lung-da* country with whom he had talked had sent many men to fetch him away by force, how for several years, the king of that country had shut him up in a room built in the 12th layer of the wall, and how he had only been able to escape by finding his golden flutes. These he blew loudly calling all the other bullocks, who came running and stamping till the ground was shaken with their tread, and the noise of their bellowing was like thunder. He told them the same story he had told *Thage*. They all rushed to the *Lung-da* country lowered their heads, and tried to toss the palace up with their horns.

The king grew very alarmed "Don't destroy my palace, he cried,' "I will give you anything you want." The bullocks answered :—" Give us your daughter who is hidden away in a room that lies in the 12th layer of one of the walls. We demand her as a ransom."

The king told them he would present her to them with one half of his Kingdom, only they themselves would have to leave the country.

They left in great state, the Princess had eight women-attendants on her left-hand side, and eight male attendants on her right.

When they had come back to the jungle, the bullocks built a palace for the Prince and the *Lung-da* Princess. It was so high up that the *Rum* country was but an elbow length away, and as it hung in the air, it was far above the ground. A great feast was given, much '*chi*' was drunk, and the land was called *Jambo-lha*, the bullocks made thrones for the orphan boy and his wife, who became king and queen of that country.

And in that valley, we Rong-folk believe the best butter and milk can be obtained.

II. LAP-CHA CUSTOMS.

(*a*). Family Life.

In defining the family life of a Lap-cha, a brief description will be given of his cottage with the village he lives in. A Rong-folk hamlet generally consists of sixteen cottages, standing on or near the ground the owners cultivate. *Din-lok* at *Sing-tom* has told me that this number ensures help and comfort, but whether this number has any superstitious belief, I have been unable to discover. There is usually a Buddhist temple and monastery where the *lamas* reside. The *mandal* or village headman is the man who attends to order, punishing trivial misdemeanours himself, and reporting serious affairs to the nearest town where a judge holds a court every six or eight months.

The Lap-cha builds his cottage from the woody stems of a bamboo (the *po*). The building is raised six feet from the ground and supported by wooden pillars that are fastened to stones placed just below the ground. The plaster forming the walls is made from the bamboo stem (*fyung*) that is mixed with mud, while the steps leading up to the rooms are just a notched bamboo trunk, being the same kind of bamboo that is used for the framework of the building. The thatch that makes the roof is of a small bamboo (*prong*), which is placed in between the larger stems of the same plant that are split from node to node.

Life in a Lap-cha hut is very simple. The family wakes when the cock crows, and rises when they hear the hens underneath the building jump down from their perches. After they have washed their hands and faces, and should the hut contain a Buddhist altar, they fill the seven bowls with water (else the god would be considered thirsty), bow down three times in front of it, and chant reverently the Lamaistic formula of worship "*Om mani pe-me hum chi,*" (Hail! the jewel in the lotus). Then they drink (*chi*) and eat rice (*zo*) and after feed the animals and the fowls. Then they all go to work in the fields, first sharpening their knives, (*ban*) on a stone slab. The remains of the breakfast are taken with them which they finish when hungry. In the evening they collect weeds, leaves, ferns, vegetables, fruit and yams and return home. The men of the house sit down to rest, while the women either make sour buckwheat bread from the plant called *ka-hru-khu,* or sweeter bread from flour, which is called *ka-hret-khu,* or boil Indian corn (*kung chum*). The women give the men '*chi,*' also taking it themselves; while supper consists of the same food they had in the morning. The bowls of water on the altar are emptied. It is believed that were this not done, the water would turn to blood, and a lamp is placed on the altar. This is a small brass bowl that comes from Tibet, and is lighted by means of a small piece of bamboo being lit that is wound round with cotton and floats in butter or mustard-oil. For light in the building itself, now modern lamps filled with kerosene oil are used. Poor families have just the burning sticks they take from their hearths.

Family quarrels are unusual and in the case of a village feud, people avoid each other. '*Chi*'-drinking causes fights when the Lap-cha uses his hands, and though he may use a stick, he never uses his knife (*ban*), which he always has with him, and the morning finds them joyful.

(*b*) Birth.

Virgin birth is only connected with folk-tales in Sikhim. There seem to be no legends of a son 'beautiful as a celestial' whose father was the Sun-god, like we read of in the Mahabharata. The woman who expects a child must not eat the flesh of any animal whose throat has been cut, from the fifth month. If she does, the child will be born with a red mark round its neck and he will die. An animal must not either be eaten that has been killed in her presence. Should the woman by any mistake have eaten of an animal who was killed in this manner, the bones are kept until the child is born and are then rubbed on his throat. Distorted plantains that are twisted and out of shape must not be eaten by the woman or else it is believed the child's fingers and toes will resemble them. Should the basket she carries fall off her back when containing food, she may not eat any of the contents. She is also expected to lead a quiet homely life and not go out at night lest the child die. Women at that time go often to a river and protect themselves against evil spirits by sacrificing two fowls.

The husband at that time may not ride, he must not touch a pony or even a saddle and bridle. Should he do so, it may be twelve months before the child is born and in that case the woman will be sure to die.

Although couvade existed formerly in the south of India, very few traces of the custom are to be found in Sikhim. In some cases I heard of a man going into seclusion for ten days before the birth of his child. During those days he lives in another room of the cottage, ignoring his wife completely, but he sees she has the best food and that she is well attended. This they say is an incentive to bring good-luck, and it is frequently mentioned in folk-tales.

The *lamas* in the village give pregnant women a stone having the shape of a *dorje* (a thunderbolt) from which paste is made which they eat. It is supposed to facilitate child-birth.[1]

---

[1] The following story was given at Tumun, (great superstition is attached to a thunderbolt, and a 'dorje' in brass, is the religious symbol

Should the husband be a *lama* he utters prayers for one night in the Tibetan language, while a '*mun*'[1] is called in to make sacrifices to propitiate the evil demons. A cock or a hen is frequently offered, but should the demon be not appeased, he is called the *gyek-rum* and is turned into a god in order to conciliate, whilst a pig is also given him! The friend who is called in to help receives Rupee one and two yards of cloth. Frequently the woman goes into the wood to have a child, thus leaving everything to nature.

The duration of uncleanness is one month. After then the position of the woman in the village improves considerably, the mother of a child having more authority.

The child is visited by a *lama* after three days, who prepares a horoscope telling the parents how long the child will live, how often he will be ill, and whether he will be lucky or unlucky. He also names him, choosing the day of the week on which he is born. Thus a boy may be called *Posa* meaning *Friday*, whilst the parents choose the name *Potet*. The parents receive their name from the first child, and if the son were called *Posa-Potet* the father would be *Posa-Potet-bo* (father), while the mother would be known as *Posa-Potet-mo*, the language being teknonymous.

Directly the child is born butter is placed in his mouth and after one hour ground rice is given to him. It is considered unlucky for a child to be born with long hair or having teeth, as it means the father and mother will both die that year.

Boys are weaned after three years, and girls after four. During teething the child is taken great care of, and the mother may not eat salt, drink '*chi*,' or have anything that has acid in it.

When a child is very ill, a *Mun* is called in to sacrifice to the demons. When the child recovers it is said she has cured it. The demons are supposed to send disease, and the one who sends small-pox is known as the *rum-du*. Tetanus is believed to be caused by touching the image of a god, e.g., the Buddha that is found on household altars.

Deformed children are instantly killed, the mother in a case

---

of a *lama*): 'Once upon a time, an orphan boy went over the hill and fell over a steep precipitous rock. It was twilight and he fell into a pig-sty landing on the back of a pig. Then it commenced to thunder so that he shook with fright. One report was so loud that it reverberated and sent the boy to the top of the mountain once more. So it is a Lap-cha fable that a pig is the cause of thunder and we never laugh at it. A horse, dog, cow and goat must not be laughed at either. If they are it may cause thunder and lightning, and should a tree ever be struck, the form of a '*sa-dar*' is always found underneath it, though it is only made of stone. The '*sa-dar*' is the Demon of Lightning, and is always carved on a Buddhist altar, being eight feet high. It is represented as a dragon holding three precious stones (*norpu*) in his claws.

[1] See note to I. folk-lore of the Rong-folk.

of that sort being well treated by her husband but badly by her neighbours. Insanity is said to be caused through a demon's presence in a child. The villagers say, "*Mung-suk* the demon has him."

If a child dies when he is under five years old, he is placed in a box under some stones on the mountain side as it is said he is too young to bear the weight of the earth. A little soil is put round the spot which is fenced round. After three days the place is visited, and the foot-marks on the soil noticed, which show the relatives if the child has re-incarnated into a human person again or another animal. If no marks are observed the relatives believe the child has gone to play with its ancestors in Heaven (the *rum-lyang*). If the child is a boy, he wears a pair of short knickers made from a species of nettle called the *sa-hrong*. This is first soaked and then dried with ashes over it making the pulpy substance fall off, and the fibre is used as thread. A girl wears a cloth of the same material fastened over her shoulder with a bamboo pin. A belt is also worn that is made from the bark of a fruit tree (the *kun-pot*). A cradle is never used, the baby sleeps on the floor wrapped in a blanket, and when carried is placed in the *kasok*, the pouch-like fold a woman makes with the end of her garment and that is tucked into her belt. When older, the child is carried on the back and fastened with a long piece of cloth. He never wears any head-dress.

The Lap-cha has few toys. Boys only play with leaves and mud. The girls play with a doll (*a-kup dim*) made from the leaves of a kind of lemon, the *kan-tu*, that are rolled together and tied in the centre with a piece of fibre. It is always feminine and rejoices in the name of "*maim*" which means a lady.

A woman or a man will never touch a doll when they are expecting a child, as it is believed he might be dumb or sightless. Boys when older make a small flute called a *pa-lit* which is also made from the bark of the fruit tree, *kun-pot*. Children's clothes are thrown away after their death in order to prevent unhappy reminders.

A boy wears a lucky necklace which comes from Tibet as an amulet. It contains three beads only, one long black one and two coral. The girl wears an amulet having many beads, five long black ones and several coloured ones. She also wears a bracelet which a boy does not, but they both wear ear-rings even when they are very small, but a Lap-cha woman never has her nose pierced or wears anklets.

The birth of a girl for the first child is considered very lucky, as a girl helps the parents much more than a boy, who plays the whole time.

The *Rum* are supposed to take care of a child, and there are many demons who would harm him. The *sung-grong-mung* is the name of the demon who steals little children. If a baby sucks a thumb or big toe it is considered lucky, but should it suck nothing at all it is unlucky. Should a child cry it means he is unhappy, and he gives the parents no rest. Should he however play a great deal it is considered propitious.

The Lap-cha never practises circumcision. When illegitimate children are born, the mother is known to have thrown the corpse into a river at night, thus hiding her wrong from the villagers. Bad crops are said to be a result of some one behaving wrongly and a *Mun* is required to offer sacrifices.

When a child is thrown into the river it is believed a demon takes him. I have not been able to find out whether infanticide is due to economic causes or not.

Salt is never given to small children as it is said their bones will become soft.

(c) Marriage.

The following chapter, making the group system of relationship among the Rong-folk family clear, has been made possible by using R. S. Rattray's method,[1] by which he explains how the correct inferences may be obtained. These are acquired by working out the late Dr. Rivers' system,[2] by studying Mr. Seligman's form of procedure,[3] and studying Frazer who gives valuable information on this subject, and to whose work many references are here given.[4]

The classificatory system of the Lap-cha tribe has, I believe, never been worked out, and as it is essential to give two forms of nomenclature to nearly every relation, a different term being applied to the same kinsman or kinswoman—according to their age—it has made the writing of the tables of generation very complicated.

Tremendous sexual freedom exists among the Lap-chas, and they can be described as a race having polyandry, as well as being a tribe that is polygamous. Only the law of not marrying blood relations is strictly adhered to, and severe punishment is meted out to those who break this rule. In the cases of known incest, the man and woman are sent away from the village never to return. In this connection it is interesting to note that the mother's relations are considered to be of much nearer kin than the father's. The Lap-cha believe it to be only the father who transmits bone to his offspring, while from the mother they obtain their flesh and blood.

Sir James Frazer tells us that though Tibetans and Lap-chas forbid cousins-german to marry, Bhotias confine the prohi-

---

1 See 'Ashanti,' pp. 1–44. (Rattray.)
2 See *Kinship and Organization* (Frazer)
3 See *Man*, April 1921.
4 *Folk-lore in the Old Testament*, vol. ii, pp. 94–371.

bition to cousins on the father's side, and more particularly to the children of the father's brother. The reason given is that the bone inherited from the father in this case would be pierced resulting in course of time in various infirmities.

Among the Lap-cha three brothers can marry three sisters, and all the wives are common. In such a case the children of the eldest girl belong to the eldest brother, while those of the youngest sister belong to the youngest brother. Should one or more of the women not bear children, the children are apportioned by arrangement, with certain restrictions, which will be described later. Two men who are not related may have one wife, but this is unusual.

A man occasionally lends a wife to a visitor. In the ante-married state of the girl, virginity is not considered essential. Should she have a child and if he is a good worker, it is considered a valuable factor. An unmarried girl becomes a nun, she lives in seclusion for three years being taught to read and write by some woman. Her tuition is paid for by her parents and by those of the boy who would have married her. After learning she attends a Buddhist monastery for the whole day three times a month.

Girls marry from the age of puberty.

Occasionally a forcible abduction takes place. Should a man's wife run away, the husband is compensated by the wife's parents, who give him back half the sum he paid for her.

A man when courting, gives the girl of his choice some handkerchiefs, and a few pieces of soap; a refusal of marriage is considered unlucky for him. As the bride-price the boy works in the girl's father's fields for one or two years, and unless he can pay the full amount they ask for their daughter then, and present them with a large brass pot, he must work for another year.

In a case I investigated personally, the son had to pay Rs. 300 for his bride, and yet had to work for three years for his father-in-law.[1] The man is allowed to cohabit with the girl; sometimes children are born before the man brings his wife home.

Similar customs are observed among the tribes in Indo-China, which probably have an ethnological connection with the Lap-chas, the husband being treated more or less as a slave, and his services considered an economic factor.

The custom among the Lap-chas is that should a man pay but a small amount for his wife, he will have to work for a longer period, though for several years after he helps his father-in-law in his fields in harvest time.

In the *Rong*-tribe in order that a marriage may be arranged, two go-betweens are required, one acting for each family. They introduce the subject first of all by visiting the girl's parents

---

[1] The eldest son of the Ate lama in Tumun.

and presenting them with a brass water-vessel. Should the parents accept this gift, the purpose of the visit is disclosed, and a day is fixed when they will come with the boy to introduce him. On the appointed day, the two go-betweens arrive with the boy, who brings with him a pig and a roll of white cloth from Assam. They also place several rupees before the parents, which is eventually deducted from the bride-price, and which varies according to the wealth of the boy. They bring a big copper pot to cook the food in, and a brass pot to boil '*chi.*' The drink is then made and a great feast is given to which all the villagers are invited. The young man brings a cock with him which he and the bride eat.[1] A year passes and then it is the turn of the boy's parents to give a feast. The go-betweens come with the boy to fetch the girl from her home. The parents do not follow her as it is considered unlucky were they to go with their daughter. This time it is the girl who brings a pig with her and a basket of '*chi.*' The boy's family kill two bullocks, one pig and seven fowls, and before eating offerings of food and drink are made to the *Rum.*

The *lamas* and the village headman drink the health of the bride and bridegroom and are witnesses to the marriage, this being the only legal proceeding that is taken. At these feasts the girl sits between a '*nyom-mu*' and a '*nyom-byng.*' These are two sisters, generally of the mother—handmaidens they could be termed—the '*nyom-mu*' must, however, be married. They receive the remains of the bride-price which they give to the parents. That night, the visitors sing and dance till the day breaks, stamping their feet on the floor. (There is only sorrow when the bride leaves her home.) The mother cries while the father gives her advice saying:—"Be nice to your husband's people, and work hard for them, remember we have sold you to them—". For one week, the bride from supposed shyness does no work in her husband's home, but after seven days, she works in the house and the fields. Should she have some children already, they are taken over by the husband.

The marriage tie is very slight, and can be theoretically

---

[1] *Nam* is a year in Lap-cha, the new year is *nam-bu*, which varies according to the date of the new moon, and according as the period is altered by the addition of an intercalary month. See Mainwaring, Grammar of the Rong (Lepcha) language, (Calcutta 1876), p. 141. Marriage rules vary in every village, in some cattle is never exchanged, in others the bridegroom brings his future parents a bullock and the bride is given a cow. The custom alters with the wealth of the families. In some cases the bridegroom may bring a cock, while the bride takes a hen to her new home. When families are too poor to pay for a bride, they effect an exchange, exchanging a daughter for a wife for their son. *Pa-zu* at *Song* told me the following:—*Tikung-tek* and *Nikung-ngal* were the first two who were married; they made a golden bridge near Tibet for their wedding, which a spider helped them make, and that is why we Rong-folk give the first fruits of the harvest to them in remembrance.

dissolved at any time by the man or the woman, especially in the case of childlessness. In practice however I did not come across a single case in which divorce had taken place, even when the marriage was childless.

It is considered lucky for a man who is born in the 'bullock' year to marry a girl who is born in the 'rat' year. It is said that they will become very rich. The man in that case being either her senior by eleven years or else one year her junior.[1] It is never thought correct for the mother to stay with her daughter and son-in-law. The Lap-cha custom is for the husband to cohabit with the younger sisters of his wife during the lifetime of his wife, and even should they be married.

These two customs, that Frazer has termed the Sororate and the Levirate, are observed in different tribes in many parts of the world, and it is curious to note that a Lap-cha man may marry the *younger* sister of his wife, though he can only cohabit with the wife of his *elder* brother. But though the custom of marrying in the order of seniority is usually observed in connection with Sororate and Levirate practices, it is not customary among the Rong-folk.

(*a*) Table I.—The elder brother's wife is common to all the brothers, and should the second brother take a wife she is common to all the brothers younger than himself. The eldest brother is not allowed to cohabit with the wives of his younger brothers. It is only the wife of the youngest brother with whom no one can have access. Should the younger brother die, his wife returns home, marrying generally into another family; she may not live with any of her late husband's elder brothers. Hence the nomenclature for sisters is extensive: *nom-ren-bo* meaning the eldest sister (*ren*-eldest), *nom-hlen-bo* means the second eldest sister (*hlen*-between), whilst *nom-byek-bo* means the third elder sister, and *nom-chum-bo* is the name given to the youngest (*chum*-younger).

It is the youngest brother who has the monopoly of his wife, though it is hard to understand if this has any claim to ultimogeniture, inheritance of '*nasti*' and fields being divided amongst all the brothers who live together. Thus though a man may live with his brothers' wives, should the brothers be older than himself, he could not cohabit with his younger brother's wife, who is called a *nyom* meaning bride. The best view to take, it seems, is to adopt Frazer's opinions on the subject which he explains so clearly in the systems of the Sororate and Levirate. He thinks they are made clear by studying the terms

[1] A woman is never allowed to mention the name of her son's wife, who, never in return, can pronounce the name of her mother-in-law. The mother calls her by the name of her first child, thus should the child be called *Guruck* (*Curly-locks*), the daughter-in-law is called *Guruck-bo*, mother of *Curly-locks*). It is the same with the husband of a daughter, and with a nephew's wife or a niece's husband.

used in a tribe for the Classificatory technical names of relationship. It will be seen that the same term is applied for the man's wife as is given to his wife's sisters, *nom*; while the same term but with the masculine 'u' *num* is used for himself the husband, and the brothers. Though the term for the brothers' wives and the sisters' husbands correspond, they are not the same as the two former, being *a-ngop* or *a-zong* in each case. But it can be understood that fraternal polyandry existed in the former days, and coincided with the force of sexual communism that took place then, though it has developed among the Lap-cha into the form of marriage they now have when they must have no connection with a blood relation.

The term that is applied to the father's brothers' sons and daughters, and the mother's brothers' sons and daughters is *a-num* and *a-nom* respectively, the difference in the sex as has already been noticed being denoted by the use of a 'u' or an 'o,' but the Lap-cha is not allowed to marry his cross-cousin, though should one be a widow having no children, the matter could be gone into by a council of the village folk, who would come together and discuss it, permitting it to take place on occasions.

The father's brother's son's wife and the father's sister's son's wife have the same terms as those of the elder and younger brothers' wives. Should the husband be older than Selah, she would be called *a-ngop* or *a-zong* and he could have access to her; if however the husband were younger, she would be called or *a-nyom* and Selah would not be allowed to live with her. The same rule is also applied to the mother's brother's son's wife and to her sister's son's wife. Both the father's sister's son and the mother's brother's son are classed as *a-num* meaning brothers.

Pha-ming is an idiom in the Rong-folk language meaning the elder or younger brother, and the word *musang-mu* is another word denoting a sister of any age.

It should also be noticed that the younger brother addresses his elder brother's wife with the same term as she uses when addressing him—*a-ngop* or *a-zong*.

Should the first wife die, she can be replaced by another of her sisters, or even should she be childless the family supply the son-in-law with one of their daughters, even during her life.

(*b*) In Table II.—We note that the father's sister is termed *a-nyu* which is the term that is also applied to the mother-in-law. This rather infers that formerly Selah could have lived with his father's sister's daughter, though she is now classed with his sister—*a-nom* or *musang-mu*.

(*c*) In Table III.—We find that all in this generation are classed as ***Ti-kung***, ***Nyi-kung*** and ***Kub-zong*** which is translated as great grandfather, great grandmother, and great grandson. ***Ti-kung-tek*** is the lexicographical name for the great-great-great-grandfather, the name which is given to the progenitor of the Rong-folk in the cosmological folk-tales. *Ni-kung-ngal* is the name given to his wife in these tales, though the term *ni-kung-gnal-num* is translated as great-great-great-grandmother.

(*d*) In Table IV.—The first generation of descendants it is found that Seleh calls his sons-in-law *myok*, which is the same term that is applied to his youngest brother. His daughters-in-law with whom of course he has no access to, are termed *nyom*, a bride, the same term that is applied to his younger brother's wife. Their children are called *num-kun* irrespective of sex, which mean nephews and nieces. The mother's children's children are termed *kun-zong*, meaning grandsons and granddaughters, while they would term Selah their *a-koo* (uncle). The same nomenclature is used meaning the mother's brother's children's children.

(*e*) In Table V.—Which is the third generation of descendants, all the terms are *nyi-tha* or *nyi-tho*, (grandson and granddaughter), and *a-zo* (grandfather).

(*f*) In Table VI.—The generation of Selah's wife is given. It is here we note that he can marry his wife's younger sister.

A widow can marry one year after her husband's death, when as they say: "his body has turned to ashes." If the husband were a younger brother, the widow returns home with her children. When she re-marries, the man has to pay half the usual bride-price working for one year only. If her children are small, she takes them to her new home with her; if however they are big, she leaves them at home to look after the grandparents.

When two are living together who have no right to, a *lama* called a *set-suma* is called in as soon as the fact is discovered, to blow a white shell horn to prevent hail-stones and rain, and to appease the demon *Rum-si* who lives in rocks.

Table 1.—(*s*) *Selah's Generation.*

English. — Abbr. husband h, wife w, father f, mother m, daughter d, brother b, sister s, elder e, younger y.

Lap-cha. — Abbr. elder e, younger y, Marriageable M. Not to be married N.

Term	Reciprocal	(elder) Term	(younger)	(e.) Reciprocal	(y.)
Husband	Wife	Num	A-vo	Nom	A-yu
Elder brother	Younger brother	A-num or	num-fren	Num-hlep-bo or	Ing
Elder sister	Younger brother	A-nom or	nom-fren	Num-hlep-bo or	Ing
Elder b's w.	Husband's y's b.	A-ngop or	A-zong M.	A-ngop or	A-zong
Younger b's w.	Husband's y. b.		Nyom N.		A-num
Elder s's h.	Wife's y. b.		A-zong		A-zong
Younger s's h.	Wife's e. b.		Myok		A-num
Father's b's son	Father's b's son	A-num	Ing	A-num	Ing
Father's b's son's w.	Husband's f's b's son	A-ngop M	Nyom N.	A-num	Ing
Father's b's d.	Father's b's son	A-nom or musangmu	Ing N.	A-num-pha-ming	Ing
Father's b's d's h.	Wife's f's b's son	A-zong	Myok	A-num	Ing
Father's s's son	Mother's b's son	A-num	Ing	A-num	Ing
Father's s's son's w.	Husband's f's b's son	A-ngop M.	Nyom N.	A-num	Ing
Father's s's d.	Mother's b's son	A-nom or musangmu	Ing N.	A-num-pha-ming	Ing
Father's s's d's h.	Wife's m's b's son	A-num	Myok	A-num	Ing
Mother's b's son	Father's s's son	A-num	Ing	A-num	Ing
Mother's b's son's w.	Husband's f's s's son	A-ngop M.	Nyom N.	A-num	Ing
Mother's b's d.	Father's s's son	A-nom M.	Ing N.	A-num	Ing
Mother's b's d's h.	Wife's f's s's son	A-zong	Myok	A-num	Ing
Mother's s's son	Mother's s's son	A-num	Ing	A-num	Ing
Mother's s's son's w.	Husband's m's s's son	A-zong N.	Nyom N.	A-zong	A-zong
Mother's s's d.	Mother's s's son	A-nom N.	Ing N.	A-num	Ing
Mother's sister's d's h.	Wife's m's s's son	A-zong	Myok	A-zong	A-zong

Table II.—(b) 1st Generation of Ascendants.

(Abbr. man speaking, man s. woman speaking, woman s.).

English.		Lap-cha.	
Term	Reciprocal	e. Term y.	Reciprocal
Father	Son	A-bo	Tagri-kup
F's brother	B's son	A-kon	Nam-kup
F's b's wife	H's b's son	A-nyu m.	Nam-kup
F's sister	B's son	A-nyu n.	Nam-kup
F's s's husband	W's b's son	A-zong	Nam-kup
Mother	Son	A-mu	Tagri-kup
M's brother	Son's son (man s.)	A-zyong	Kup-zong
M's b's wife	H's s's son	A-nyu	Nam-kup
M's sister	S's son (woman s.)	Mutim m. A-nyu m.	Kup-zong
M's s's husband	W's s's son	Butim A-zyong	A-kup

Table III.—(c) 2nd Generation of Ascendants.

F's father	Son's son	Thi-kung	Kub-zong
F's f's brother	S's son's son.	Thi-kung	Kub-zong
F's mother	Son's son	Nyi-kung	Kub-zong
F's f's b's wife	H's b's son's son	Nyi-kung	Kub-zong
F's f's sister	Son's son's son	Nyi-kung	Kub-zong
F's f's s's husband	W's b's son's son	Thi-kung	Kub-zong
M's mother	Daughter's son	Nyi-kung	Kub-zong
M's father	Daughter's son	Thi-kung	Kub-zong
M's m's brother	S's d's husband	Thi-kung	Kub-zong
M's m's b's wife	H's s's d's child	Nyi-kung	Kub-zong
H's m's sister	S's d's child	Nyi-kung	Kub-zong
H's m's s's husband	W's s's d's son	Thi-kung	Kub-zong

Table IV.—(d) 1st Generation of Descendants.

English.		Lap-cha.	
Term	Reciprocal	Term	Reciprocal
Son	Father	Tagri-kup	A-bo
Daughter	Father	Tayu-kup	A-bo
Son's w.	H's father	Nyom n.	A-fyat
D's husband	W's father	Myok	A-fyat
E. b's son	F's y. brother	Num-kup	A-ku-chum-bo
E. b's son's wife	H's f's y. b.	Nyom n.	A-fyat
E. b's daughter	F's y. brother	Num-kup	A-ku-chum-bo
E. b's d's husband	W's f's y. brother	Myok	A-fyat-chum-bo
Y. b's son	F's e. brother	Num-kup	Bu-tim
Y. b's son's wife	H's f's brother	Nyom n.	A-fyat
Y. b's daughter	F's s's brother	Nok-kup n.	Bu-tim
Y. b's daughter's h.	W's f's brother	Myok	A- fyat
Y. s's son	M's e. brother	Ing	A-zyong
Y. s's daughter	M's e. brother	Nom-kup	A-zyong
S's son's wife	H's m's brother	Nyom n.	A-num or a-fyat
S's d's husband	W's m's brother	Myok	A-num or a-fyat
M's s's daughter's son	M's m's s's son	Kup-zong	A-koo
M's s's daughter's d.	M's m's s's son	Kup-zong	A-koo
M's s's d's son's w.	H's m's m's s's son	Nyom n.	A-koo
M's s's d's d's husband	W's m's m's s's son	Myok	A-fyat
M's b's son's son.	F's f's s's son	Kup-zong	A-koo
M's b's son's d.	F's f's s's son	Kup-zong	A-koo
M's b's d's d.	M's f's s's son	Kup-zong	A-koo
M's b's son's son's wife	H's f's f's s's son	Nyom n.	A-fyat
M's b's son's d's h.	W's f's f's s's son	Myok	A-fyat
M's b's d's son's wife	H's f's f's s's son	Nyom n.	A-fyat
M's b's d's d's h.	W's m's f's s's son	Myok	A-fyat

Table V.—3rd Generation of Descendants.

English.		Lap-cha.			
Term	Reciprocal	e. Term	y.	e. Reciprocal	y.
Son's son's son	F's f's father	Nyi-tha		A-zo	
Son's son's d.	F's f's father	Nyi-tho		A-zo	
D's d's son	M's m's father	Nyi-tha		A-zo	
D's d's daughter	M's m's father	Nyi-tho		A-zo	
and all of this generation are the same.					

Table VI.—(f) Genealogy of Selah's wife.

W's brother	Sister's husband	A-num-mu	Zong-mu	A-num	A-ngop or a-zong
W's b's wife	H's s's h.	A-num-mu-zong		Num-mu-zong	
Wife's sister's	S's husband	A-num		A-num	A-ngop or a-zong
Ascendants.					
Wife's father	Daughter's h.	A-fyat		Myok	
Wife's mother's	Daughter's h.	A-nyu		Myok	
Descendants.					
W's b's son	F's s's h.	Num-kup		Num-mu-zong	
W's b's daughter	F's s's h.	Num-kup		A-zyong	
W's s's son	M's s's h.	Num-kup		A-zyong	
W's s's son's wife	H's m's s's h.	Nyom		A-zyong	
W's s's daughter	M's s's h.	Num-kup		A-zyong	
W's s's d's husband	W's m's s's h.	Myok		A-fyat	

(*d*). Death and Burial.

Men and women who have always been true to the "*Sang-yo*," i.e. to the holy works and sacred rites of Buddha, are believed to join the *Rum*. Those who have been cruel and unkind and who have not acted 'according to the book' are said to go to the "*mung-lyang*," which means the land of the evil spirits, where the deceased will turn into a demon.

For three days the spirit is believed to remain with the body in the grave, a *lama* reads many prayers at that time rendering the spirit conscious, till realizing the body is dead, he (the spirit), leaves. The demon called the "*thin-myo-mung*" is said to have cut the thread of life. He is said to be a wicked man, who takes a long time dying. The death-demon is never expelled as in Lamaism proper.

A festival is given soon after death, a cow is killed and '*chi*' is made and drunk. The feast lasts for several days during which time the mourners sit and talk. On the day of burial a *lama* comes to sacrifice a goat and says to the dead :—"You are now dead, and have left this house, do not think of your wife and children, do not think of any of the animals else they will all die, and we shall know that your spirit is still here."

When a man or a woman dies, a lamp is placed above their head, hanging on a tripod. A lama is called in to say prayers, who washes him, and after tying him up in the sitting position, places him in a large copper pot (*song-fyu*). The body stays here for several days when it is carried away for burial or cremation.[1] The Rong-folk used formerly to bury their dead, but now, as Buddhist converts, they burn them and throw the ashes into a big river. A boy-*lama* termed the *khyan-no* stays by the corpse. This is given food and drink until the day of cremation: at night the food is burnt, but the drink is given to the *khyan-no*. The consequences are said to be bad if food is eaten that has lain near the dead body, with the idea that foulness has entered it with the dying man's breath.

At the grave formerly two chickens were killed, a cock and a hen. One was white, an offering to the *Rum* or gods, while the other was black in order to propitiate the *Mung* (evil demons). Two bags were hung on the fence which was built round the grave, in which the cock and hen were both placed, the white at the head, and the black one at the foot. Sometimes if the

[1] Visited a *basti* in the village of Bom near Kalimpong on September 13th and witnessed this part of the ceremony. The dead man was sitting in a brass pot, his face covered over with a white cloth and a red tape was bound round his throat tightly, which is cut just before burial or cremation. He had a rupee placed on the top of his head to appease the demon with, who would try to prevent him entering the country. At intervals they propitiated the evil-demons by burning food for them outside. I witnessed the lama talking to the dead who had food and drink given him.

family were very poor, eggs were used instead of fowls, one being smeared over with charcoal to make it black. The spirit hovers over the grave for three days, when the grave is visited, in order to tell by the foot-marks inside the fence, whether it is a human or an animal the dead have re-incarnated into. The ashes are looked at in the case of cremation.[1]

A man's re-incarnation is said not to be happy if he has been killed by wild animals. Dreams about the dead, should they be pleasant, mean that the dead have joined the *Rum*.

Should death be caused through a disease, the luck of the generation is said to have been bad (*gyit*).

If a man dies in some inaccessible spot, his clothes and his hat only are sent to the *lama* whilst his friends bury him.

(e) Miscellaneous Observances.

The Lap-cha live chiefly on agriculture and on plants and roots he finds in the jungle. Rice, paddy, Indian corn, wheat, barley, millet, etc., are cultivated, giving three or four harvests every year.[2] It appears there are no special observances in connection with these, with the exception of sacrifices to the *Rum* or to the demon who has to be propitiated.

Hunting and fishing are practised with primitive implements, poisoned arrows being used, or nets and traps made of bamboo. The *Rum* and the demons also have to be propitiated in this case. The fever the fisherman catches setting these traps is believed to have been caused through the water-spirit's displeasure.[3]

Bamboo is the chief material the implements are made of in Lap-cha life; mats, vessels, etc., even pins, and there is almost no sign of decorative art in their make.

---

[1] Cremation visited on Detut Hill near Tumun, November 30th. Before the faggots are placed on the ground for the cremation, a turtle in mud is placed in the ground. When the fire is lit it is considered auspicious should the smoke go up in a straight line, as it means the dead is going to join the *Rum* up above. A *mi-nork-bo* or workman, a butcher, cries out loud the number of faggots that are still left intact in the centre of the burning faggots. I was told if the body were not burnt by the evening (the cremation took place at 12 a.m.), the bones would be broken up by the *lamas*, who were sitting close at hand praying and drinking.

[2] Taxes are very low, though they are on an average to what a peasant earns, amounting roughly to Rs. thirteen eight annas per annum (about an English pound), which includes Rs. three from every '*basti*' claiming exemption from coolie work. This is a Government law, which expects coolies to wait for a fortnight at every '*dak*' bungalow to ensure means of transport for the traveller. Each coolie is paid six annas daily, but this price is raised for any journey over the border. The owner of a '*basti*' has also to pay two annas per mensem for every head of cattle or goat that is grazed in the jungle.

[3] The net used is called the '*yet*.' The '*tun-kun-mit*' is the name of the water-spirit.

Little can be said about their other arts, like weaving, pottery-making, spinning,[1] or painting. This latter craft is done on skins, which are first heated before being painted to enable the colours to be made fast, and is introduced from Tibet.

It is only very crude plates of black mud that are produced locally, all other pottery being imported from Nepal or other places.

Some villages manufacture a thick white paper from a nettle plant (*sa-hrong*). Various ropes, baskets, etc., are also made from jungle creepers.

With the advance of civilization however and the increase of the importance of the local 'bazaar,' these local arts become more rare, and the superstitions originally connected with them are forgotten.

Art in the strict sense of the word, such as painting, music, dancing, etc., is not developed much. Painting may be seen in temples, but it obviously follows Tibetan principles and tastes, while dancing consists of merely stamping the feet and revolving in circles after the Tibetan fashion.

Musical instruments consist of flutes of which there are three kinds,[2] and a Jews' harp. As specimens of the Lap-cha tunes, the following songs may be given :—

THE SONG OF THE CHAK-DOON-DOON BIRD (*fo*).

---

[1] Spinning is done by women and they are never parted from their spinning-rods. This is often spoken of in the folk-tales. The cloth is made from the cotton tree, the yarn being wound round the spindle which the woman holds in her hands.

[2] *Pa-lit; po-tong; lung-tang pa-lit.*

THE SONG OF THE BEETLE (CHYA-NYA-NYA).

CHAK DOON DOON SA VAM.

Nam toohat lat non ne, chak doon doon,
Mong zo pat to chat ka, chak doon doon,
Ka arfo lik-kang sa, chak doon doon,
Gram gram pat gat shyo, chak doon doon,
Kyo kacher tyat tachat, chak doon doon,
An ore lat non gong, chak doon doon,
Tachat ore ka, chak doon doon,
Hing book thyang gat shyo, chak doon doon,
Chang ka akyot ad yang, chak doon doon,
Arenun matlung e, chak doon doon.

SONG OF THE "*Chak doon-fo.*" (BIRD.)

The time and the season have come, *chak doon doon,*
When it is the sowing time for millet and barley, *chak doon doon,*
The pigeons cry, *chak doon doon,*
You must sow quickly, *chak doon doon.*
It is the sowing time of barley and wheat, *chak doon doon,*
When they come up, *chak doon doon,*
At that time, *chak doon doon,*

Ginger and yams will be wanted, *chak doon doon*,
Don't miss the sowing time, *chak doon doon*,
For at the end, *chak doon doon*,
You will be happy, *chak doon doon*.

CHYA-NYA-NYA-SUT.

Payong sa akong ka, chya-nya-nya,
Ore ka ho lom markhan gong, chya-nya-nya,
Kasam ore ka lom yong a, chya-nya-nya.

Pomut potong sa, chya-nya-nya,
Abong ho tyat markhan gong, chya-nya-nya,
Kasam tyat bo yong li shyong a, chya-nya-nya.

Hik boom anok num chya-nya-nya,
Boom markham na gong chya-nya-nya,
Kasam ado tandok boom yong a chya-nya-nya.

Afar agyap sa dam chya-nya-nya,
Ho ore dem Mayan gong, chya-nya-nya,
Go adom dem bo yong a, chya-nya-nya.

Chi sa tafyep a chya-nya-nya,
A sa ho lok makhan gong chya-nya-nya,
Kasam do nyet bo yong a, chya-nya-nya.

Shyang pak sa thyakam e chya-nya-nya,
Salom do tho shyong mayan na gong, chya-nya-nya,
Kasam do the be yong a, chya-nya-nya.

Shyangpak sa thyakam chya-nya-nya,
A ka ho da manan gong, chya-nya-nya,
Kasam do nyet bo yong a chya-nya-nya.

Nam bu dum atong chya-nya-nya,
A thya nun kap makhan gong, chya-nya-nya,
Go do thya bo yong a, chya-nya-nya.

THE BEETLE SONG.

The branch of the bamboo, *chya-nya-nya*.
If you cannot walk on it, *chya-nya-nya*,
Shall I walk on it for you ? *chya-nya-nya*.

The stem of the bamboo,[1] *chya-nya-nya*,
Should you not be able to cut it, *chya-nya-nya*,
Shall I cut it for you ? *chya-nya-nya*.

---

[1] *Payong*, a species of bamboo from which arrows are made, the Cephalostachyum capitatum.

If the jet-black fowl, *chya-nya-nya*,
Cannot hatch, *chya-nya-nya*,
Shall I hatch out for her, *chya-nya-nya* ?

The good thick cloth, *chya-nya-nya*,
Do you not know how to wear it, *chya-nya-nya*,
Shall I wear it for you, *chya-nya-nya* ?

The ladle, *chya-nya-nya*,
If you cannot pour from it, *chya-nya-nya*,
Shall I show you how, *chya-nya-nya* ?

The wooden pillow, *chya-nya-nya*,
Can you place the wooden blocks, *chya-nya-nya*,
Or shall I place them for you, *chya-nya-nya* ?

On it made of blocks of wood, *chya-nya-nya*,
Can you sleep on them, *chya-nya-nya*,
Or shall I show you how, *chya-nya-nya* ?

The thick woollen blanket, *chya-nya-nya*,
Can you pull it up *chya-nya-nya*,
Or shall I pull it up for you, *chya-nya-nya* ?

As has been already mentioned, the Lap-cha believes that he has an extensive demon population around him; they think that every tree and every rock is inhabited by some evil spirit. In daily life therefore the superstitions that are connected with different events are filled with details to avoid causing anger and annoyance to some demon whom they propitiate. As Buddhism, which came from Tibet, in the North, possessed such a highly developed system of demonolatry, it would be difficult to say which particular superstition—and there are many—is of genuine Lap-cha origin.

Indeed it is hard to gather much information about such observances unless one personally notices them. This is possible only when living for a long time in the midst of these people; but here several superstitions are mentioned which I came across in different villages :—

A boy had, playing one day, filled a hole under a certain tree with stones. Shortly after, a cow at home became ill, and in fear lest many humans and cattle might contract some illness, a *Mun* was immediately called in. As she prayed, the demon she was propitiating came and told her she must unblock the opening at once, or else all the cattle would die. The hole was at once freed of its contents, and the cow recovered. No one had known of the boy's deed until the *Mun* had been told of it by the demon during the ceremony.

The god of water is the *Rum-zon-pano* Sacrifices are made to him through the *Bong-thing*. An offering of fowls and eggs is given to the god, only a little being eaten while the rest is thrown into the river.

Gifts are also thrown into the river, which, like the offerings the *Bong-thing* gives, are placed in a small bamboo stem (*the pa-sun*). Two Lap-cha people wishing to be great friends always drink from the same cup. When a river has to be crossed, in order to propitiate the evil demons, leaves are at first thrown in, and when a child is carried across on its father's back, a string is thrown across the river which is supposed to take his weight (the natural phenomenon in this case being that it is supposed to produce balance).

When the *nyol* tree is cut down, its spirit is said to enter into a Lap-cha, but on no account must a piece of that wood be brought into a '*basti*,' as it means that one of the household will die.

A bullock is considered a clean animal, but when cows are milked it is said to be unlucky should anyone pass, while a few drops of their milk are always sprinkled on the ground to propitiate the evil demon *Rum-zon*. He is also spoken of as being the god who taught the Rong-folk the use of their knives, who taught them to shoot with a bow and arrow, and to kill fish. When butter is removed from the pan, a little is given to him.

In Buddhism, the house-demon is supposed to have possession on the fourth month, and amongst the Lap-cha people it is a *Mun* who, during that month, places '*chi*' on the threshold in order that he may be pacified.

Should anyone be sick, a wooden bath made from planks is made for them outside their '*basti*.' The water that is thought the most of and that is certain to affect a cure is obtained from the *Rung-fo* river (meaning the muddy-brown extended water), it is scooped up from the sides of the stream where it is rather miry and brown, and then put in the bath where it is heated by having hot stones placed in it.

In cases of sickness a dog's skull is hung over the door, and in many '*bastis*' I noticed the figure of the she-devil *Tssu-mung* over the threshold. Her form is made of a piece of dog's skull which is covered with paper that the owner of the '*basti*' has made himself. *Tssu-mung* is the demon who causes quarrelling and is always put behind prison bars represented by bamboo stems; she is surrounded by many weapons illustrating hate and discord, i.e. by spears, bows and arrows. Round her many offerings of flowers are placed which the owners hope will entice *Tssu-mung* to their hut enabling them to shut her up at once, as her touch irritates.

The threshold is never sat upon, and is stepped over. The Lap-cha believes a daughter-in-law should never carry a piece of burning wood into a hut, or it means she will have to work like a slave.

INDEX

OF SUBJECTS DEALT WITH AND NAMES OF PERSONS AND PLACES MENTIONED IN THE TALES.

Note.—The references are *to the numbers* given to the tales. The numbers in *Roman characters* being those of the *tales* themselves, while the numbers in *Arabic* figures belong to the *paragraphs* which the tales are divided into.